Covers, Sizes, & Page Counts on Kindle Direct Publishing (KDP)

Covers, Sizes, & Page Counts on Kindle Direct Publishing (KDP)

BY

TRACY WILSON

http://beautifulpublications.com

Published by
Beautiful Publications LLC
Stratford, CT 06614

©Copyright 2022 Tracy Wilson

All rights reserved. No part of this publication may be reproduced or transmitted in any form or by any means, electronic or mechanical, including photocopy, recording, or any information storage and retrieval system, without permission in writing from the copyright owner, except by a reviewer who may quote brief passages in a review.

LIBRARY OF CONGRESS CONTROL NUMBER:
2022906684

PRINT ISBN: 978-1-7356620-9-1
EBOOK ISBN: 978-1-7356620-8-4

Printed in the United States of America

This book is dedicated to everyone that needs help getting their book cover, size, & page count on KDP.

Contents

Introduction ix

"My cover designer needs my book size & page count! How can I answer this question without a book cover? Please help me!" 1

Paperback Details 2

    Paperback Content 8

    Paperback Rights & Pricing 22

Book Covers 28

Introduction

If you've already written your book and you're ready to upload your cover to KDP, then you need this book. This book will alleviate your stress as I show you how to create and upload a cover using the 'Launch Cover Creator' so that you'll be able to give your cover designer the book size & page count for your book, or you'll have the option to keep the cover you created and publish your book.

Covers, Sizes, & Page Counts on Kindle Direct Publishing (KDP)

"My cover designer needs my book size & page count! How can I answer this question without a book cover? Please help me!"

Covers, Sizes, & Page Counts on Kindle Direct Publishing (KDP)

Paperback Details

a. If you've already created your eBook in KDP, go to your eBook and click on '+Create Paperback.'

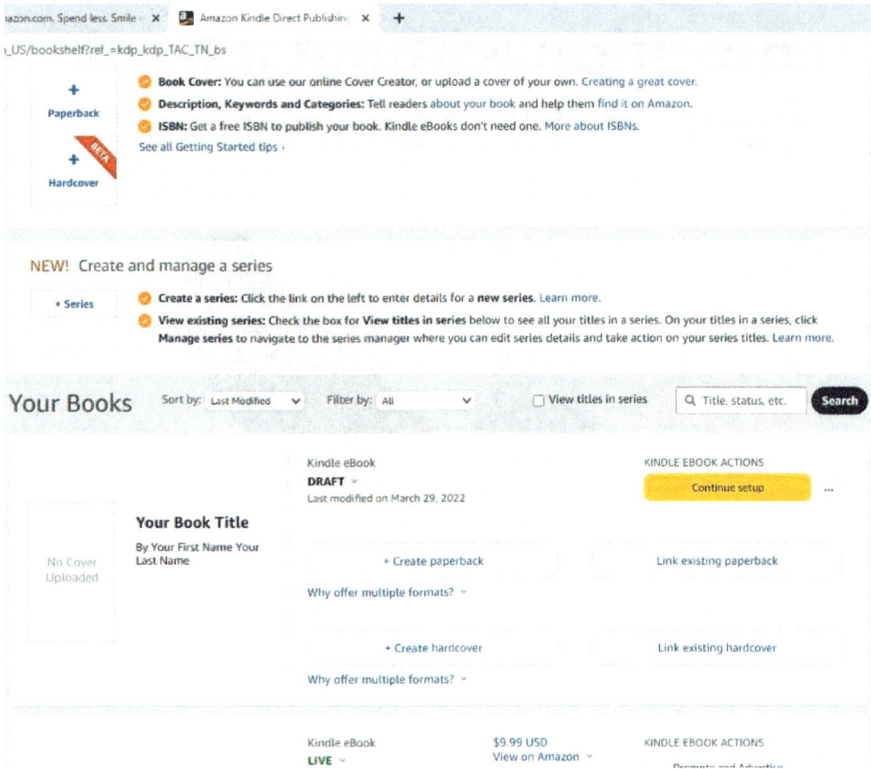

Covers, Sizes, & Page Counts on Kindle Direct Publishing (KDP)

b. If you haven't created an eBook, click on '+Paperback' under 'Create New Title' at the top of the page.

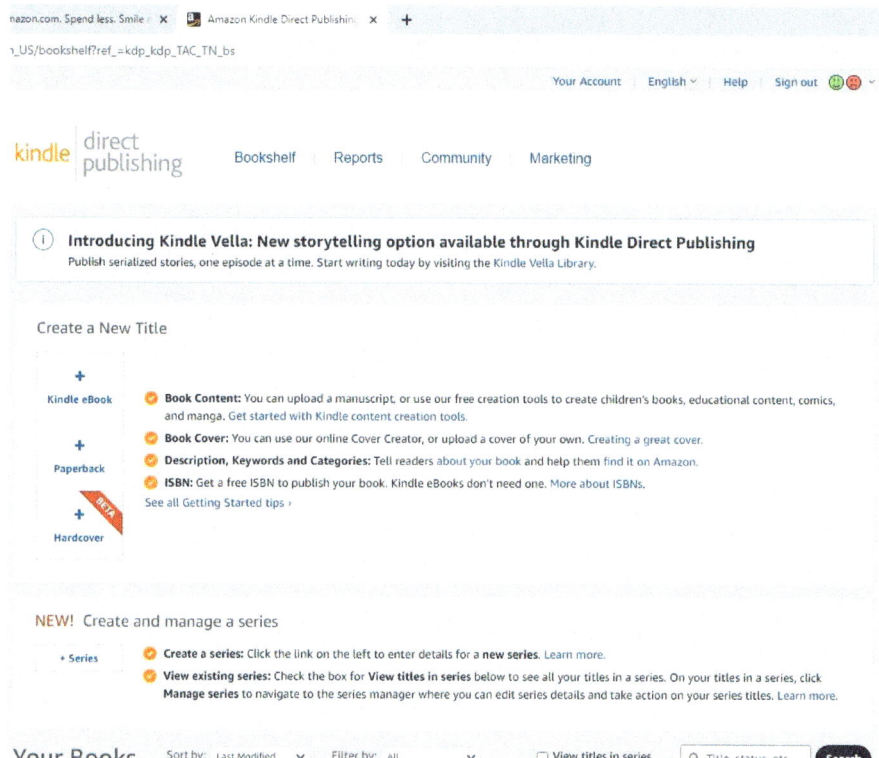

Covers, Sizes, & Page Counts on Kindle Direct Publishing (KDP)

    c. If you created an eBook first, as you scroll down you'll see the information was copied so you don't have to fill it in again. If you didn't create an eBook, you'll need to fill in the 'Book Title,' 'Author,' 'Contributors,' (if you're the only contributor leave this blank), and 'Description.'

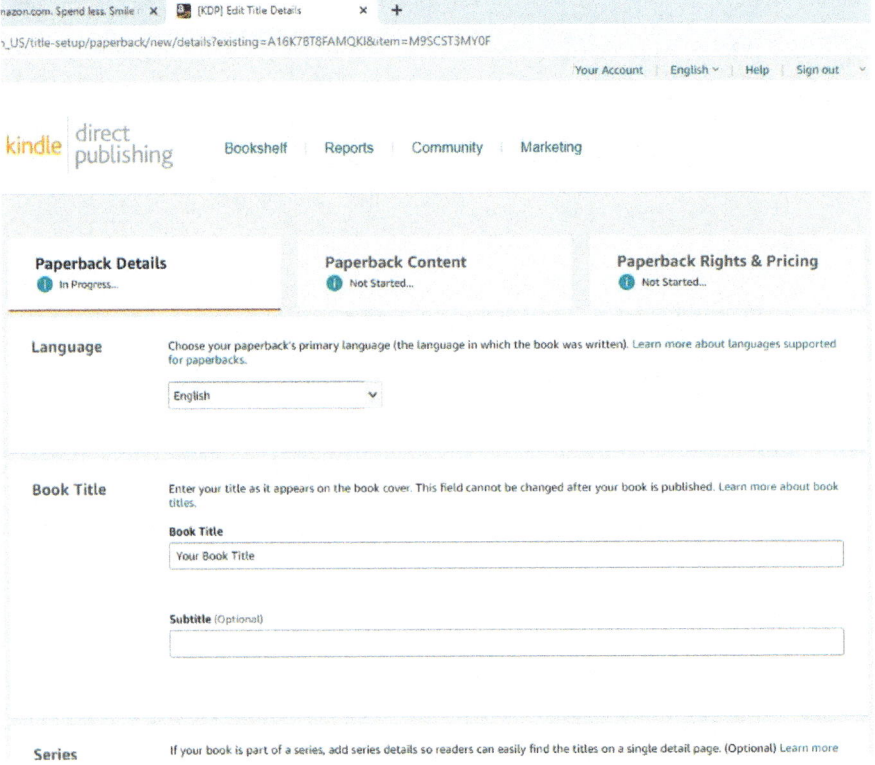

    d. Publishing Rights – always click 'I own the copyright and I hold the necessary publishing rights. You don't want to click 'This is a public domain work' because that means the copyright has expired.

4

e. Keywords – if this is your personal story, you can choose autobiography, personal story, memoir, diary, journal, childhood, marriage, family, etc. If this is fiction, there are many keywords you can choose from such as general fiction, crime, suspense, murder, mystery, detective, erotica, urban, etc.

f. Categories – click on categories and hit the plus sign next to the one you want. In this example, I clicked Nonfiction, Biography & Autobiography, and then I clicked General. I repeated the same steps and clicked Personal Memoirs. Once you're done with the categories, click on save.

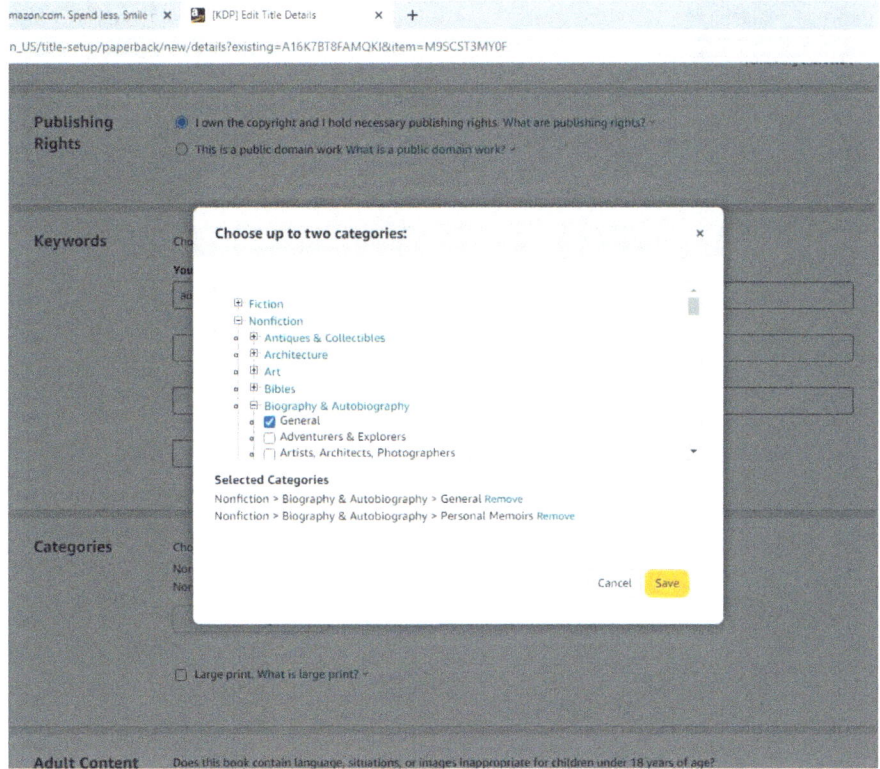

Covers, Sizes, & Page Counts on Kindle Direct Publishing (KDP)

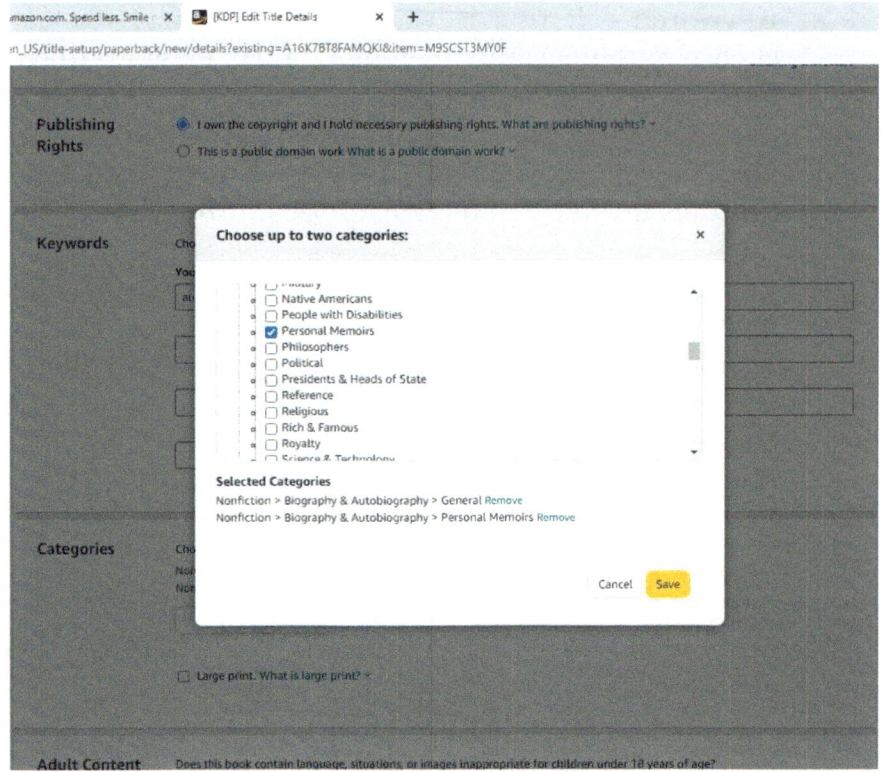

Covers, Sizes, & Page Counts on Kindle Direct Publishing (KDP)

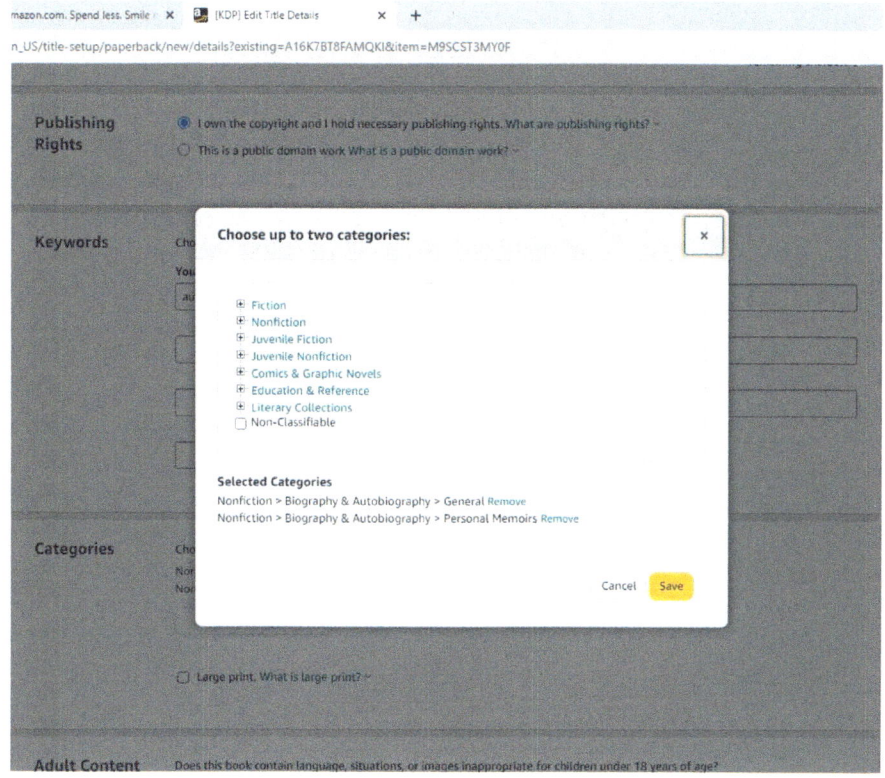

g. Adult Content – click yes or no, and click 'Save and Continue.'

7

Paperback Content

a. If you have your own ISBN, put it here. You'll need to put in the imprint to proceed. The imprint is what you used to purchase your ISBN. If you didn't purchase an ISBN, click 'Get a free KDP ISBN' and then click 'Assign me a free KDP ISBN.' You'll get a free ISBN number assigned to your book.

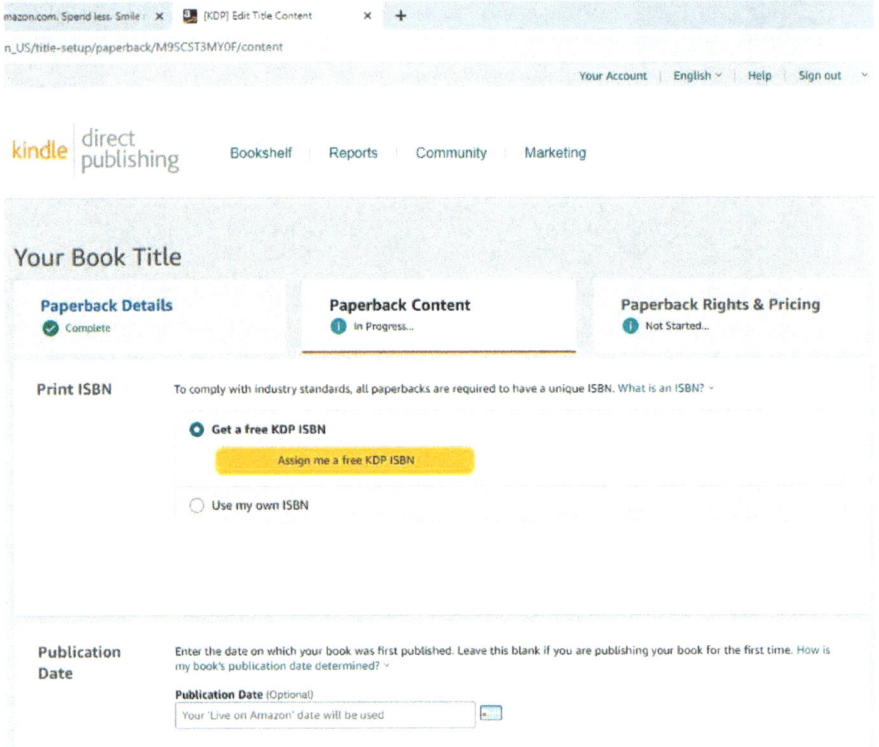

Covers, Sizes, & Page Counts on Kindle Direct Publishing (KDP)

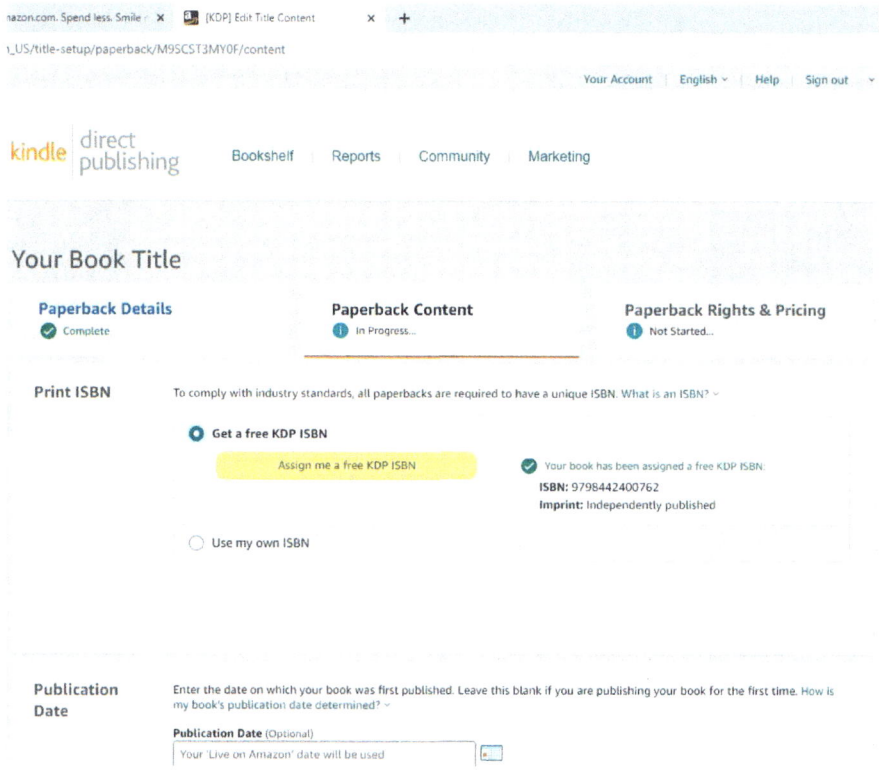

b. Publication Date – leave this blank. This will be filled in automatically once your book is published.

c. Print Options – choose the option you want. My personal preference is 'Black & white interior with white paper (this option is already highlighted).

Trim Size – 6 x 9 is highlighted but my personal preference is 5 x 8. Amazon has a lot of sizes to choose from depending on your book.

Covers, Sizes, & Page Counts on Kindle Direct Publishing (KDP)

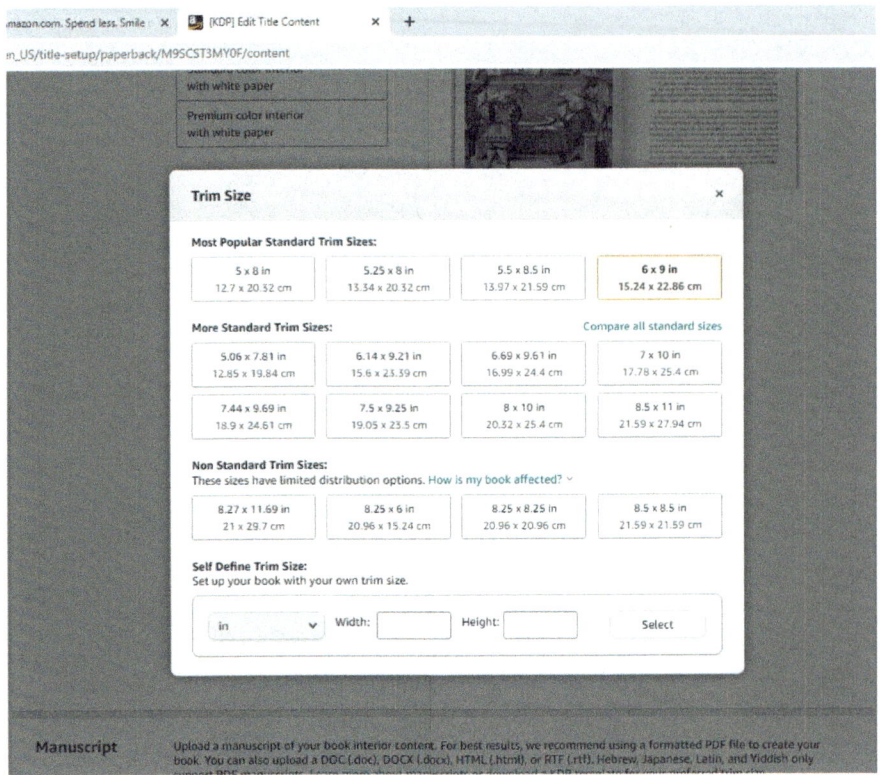

Bleed Settings – always leave the bleed settings on No Bleed.

Paperback cover finish – matte is always highlighted but I prefer Glossy.

Covers, Sizes, & Page Counts on Kindle Direct Publishing (KDP)

    d. Manuscript – here is where you upload your book. Click on 'Upload paperback manuscript' and after your folder opens, highlight your book and click 'open.'

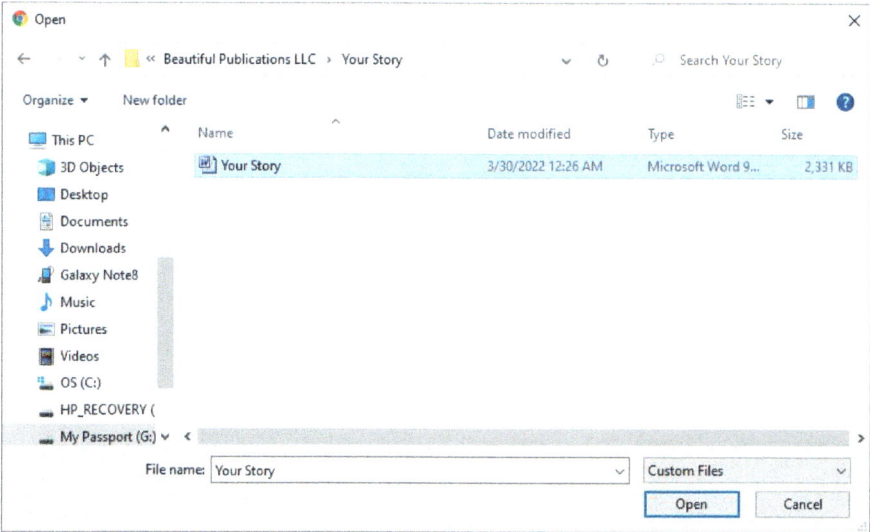

    e. Book Cover – once you see your 'Manuscript uploaded successfully!' you'll be ready to upload your book cover' however, here is where you'll need to give your cover designer the size & page count first. To do this, click on 'Launch Cover Creator.'

11

Covers, Sizes, & Page Counts on Kindle Direct Publishing (KDP)

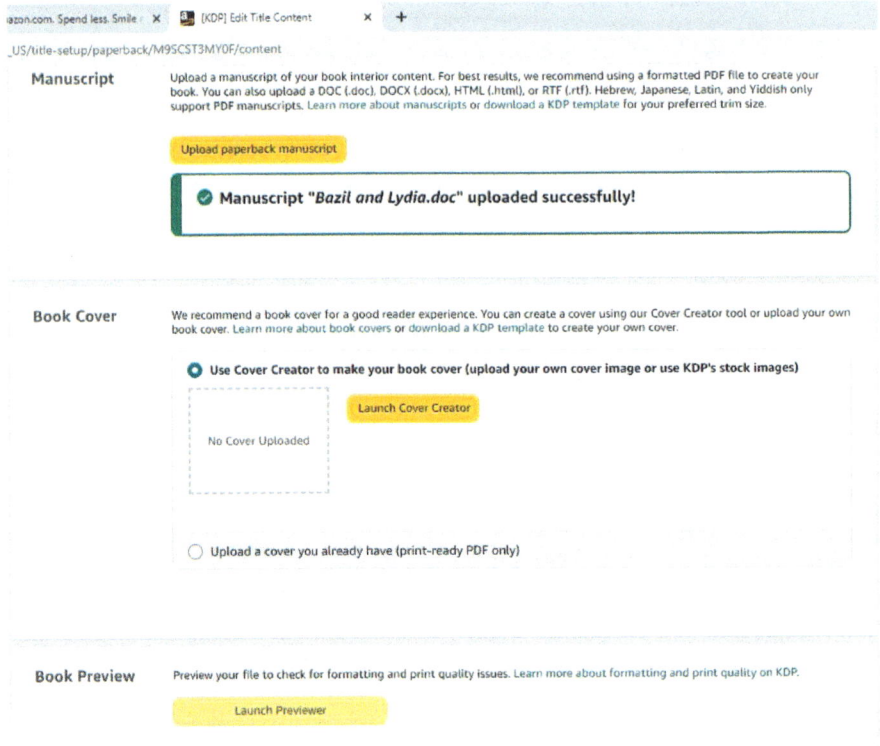

Covers, Sizes, & Page Counts on Kindle Direct Publishing (KDP)

As soon as you click on 'Launch Cover Creator' you'll get the following screen:

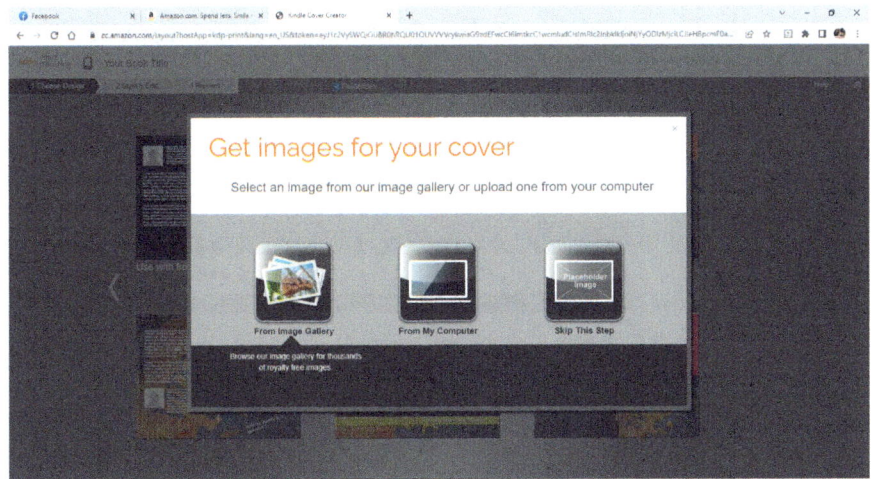

Covers, Sizes, & Page Counts on Kindle Direct Publishing (KDP)

You can click on 'From Image Gallery' or 'From My Computer.' If you click 'From Image Gallery' you'll see 'Categories' on the left. Choose a category and click on a photo. When you find an image you like, click, 'Use this image.'

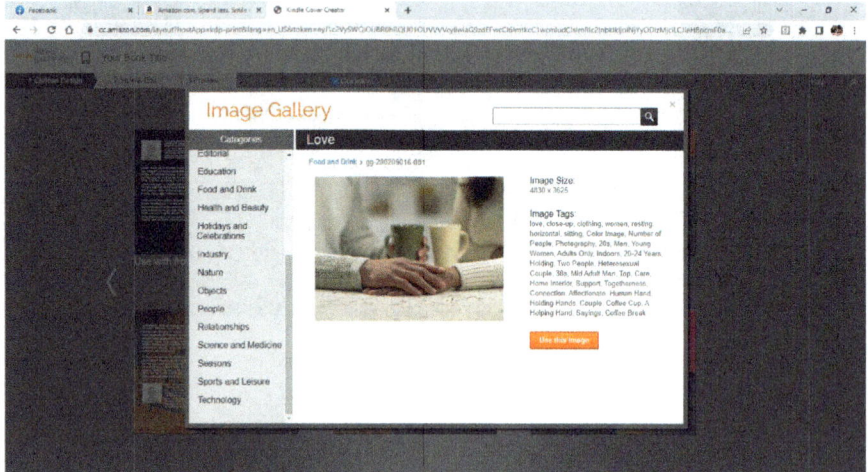

Covers, Sizes, & Page Counts on Kindle Direct Publishing (KDP)

Choose Design – pick the design you like and click 'Choose this design.'

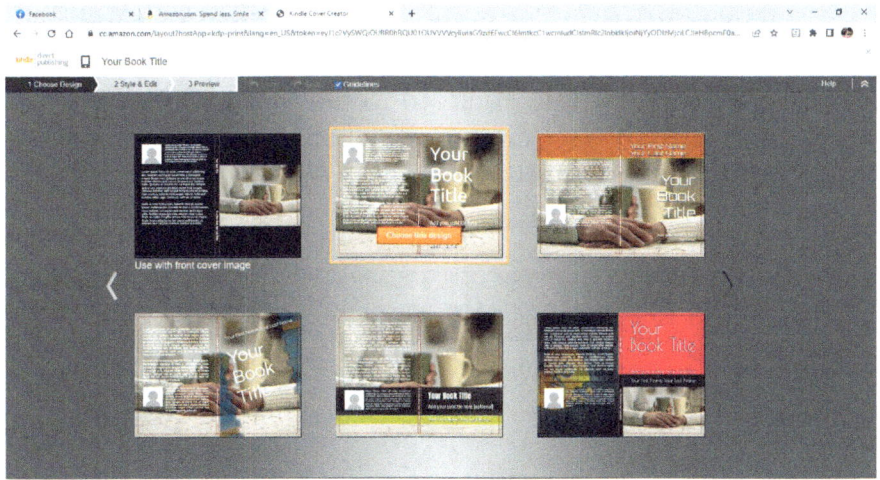

Covers, Sizes, & Page Counts on Kindle Direct Publishing (KDP)

Style & Edit – you'll be given options to upload an author photo, a biography, and a description. If you're waiting for your cover designer to send your cover, you can upload any image you want. I normally double-click to remove the biography & description section but if you're great at designing covers, you can fill these in as you like.

Covers, Sizes, & Page Counts on Kindle Direct Publishing (KDP)

Click underneath the toolbar, click save, and then click on preview.

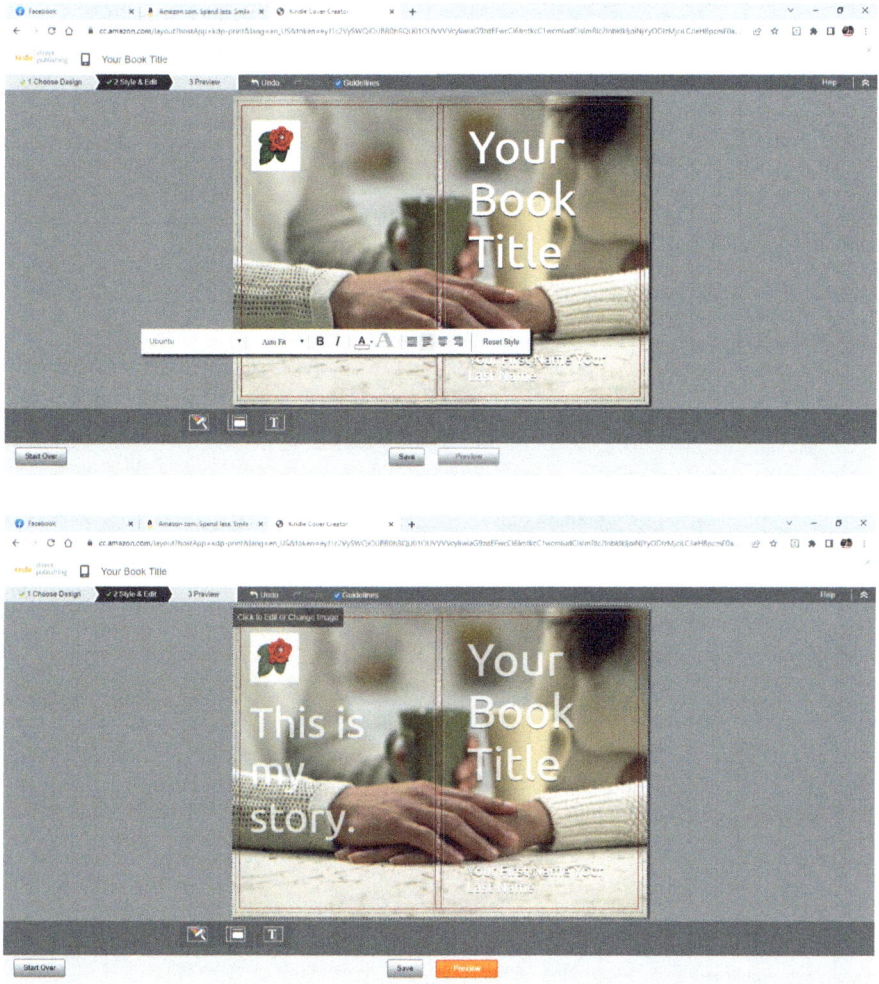

If you're waiting for your cover designer to give you a custom cover or if you're really happy with your design, click on 'Save' and submit!

17

Once you do that you'll be brought back to the 'Paperback Content' tab.

f. Scroll down towards the bottom of the page to 'Book Preview' and click on 'Launch Previewer.'

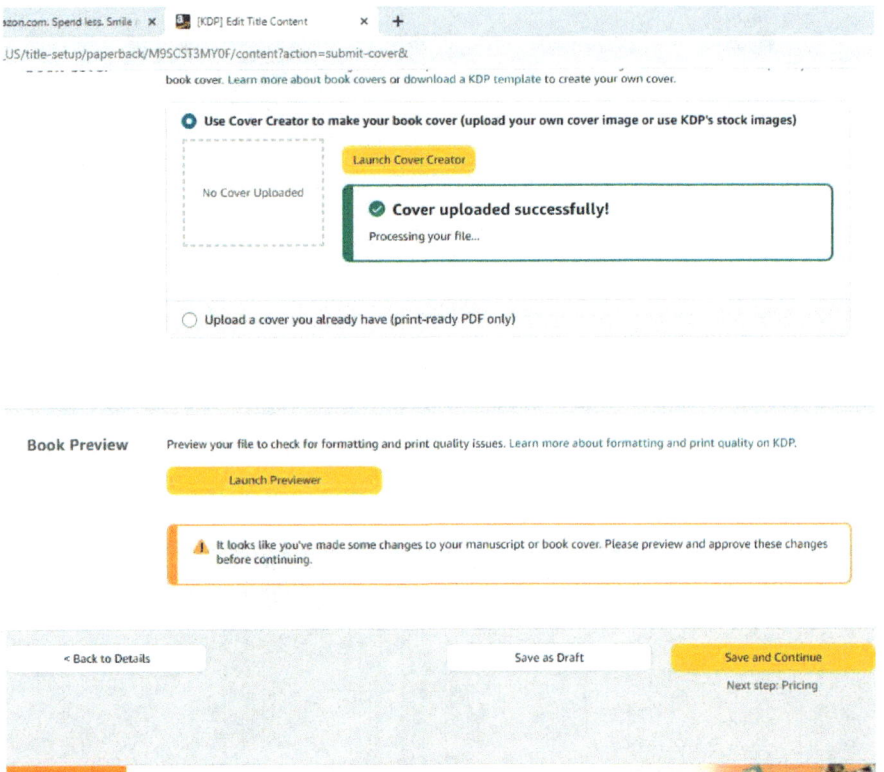

Covers, Sizes, & Page Counts on Kindle Direct Publishing (KDP)

After KDP saves, checks for quality issues, etc., you'll see the 'Print Previewer.'

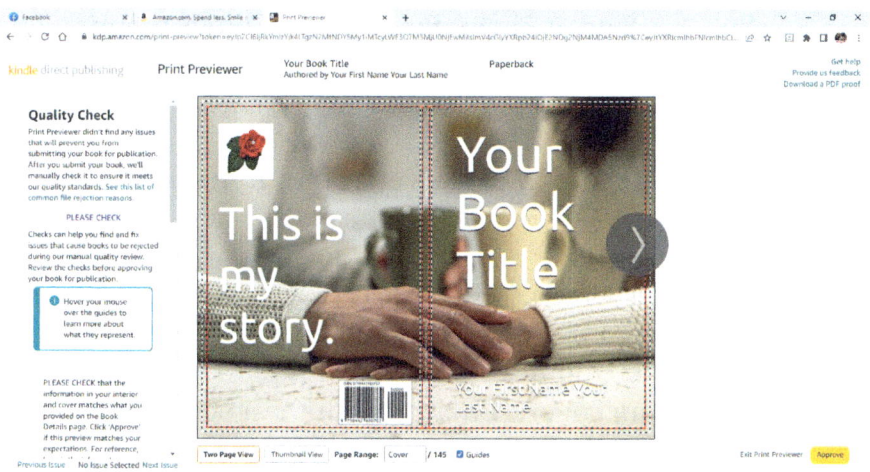

At the bottom of the page you see 'Two Page View' highlighted, 'Thumbnail View,' 'Page Range Cover/145,' and a checkmark near 'Guides.' In this example, if you're waiting for your cover designer to give you a custom cover, you'll tell them the size of your book, and you'll tell them the book is 145 pages. If you want to scroll through your book to see how it will look in print, click on the arrow above to scroll through the book. You'll see on the bottom 'Page Range: 145'. If you're waiting on your cover designer to give you a custom cover, click on 'Exit Print Previewer,' scroll down to the bottom of the page, click 'Save as Draft,' and log out. You'll come back to this page to upload your custom cover after you receive it.

19

Covers, Sizes, & Page Counts on Kindle Direct Publishing (KDP)

Now that you've received your custom cover from your cover designer, log back into your KDP account and click on the 'Paperback Content' tab. Scroll down to where you see 'Launch Cover Creator' and click 'Upload a cover you already have (print-ready PDF only). Once you click on that, you'll see the following:

'Check this box if the cover you're uploading includes a barcode. If you don't check the box, we'll add a barcode for you.' If you purchased your own ISBN a bar code was generated. If your cover designer added your bar code to your book cover, make sure you check this box. In this example I'm going to use my custom cover, 'Bazil & Lydia Osgood.'

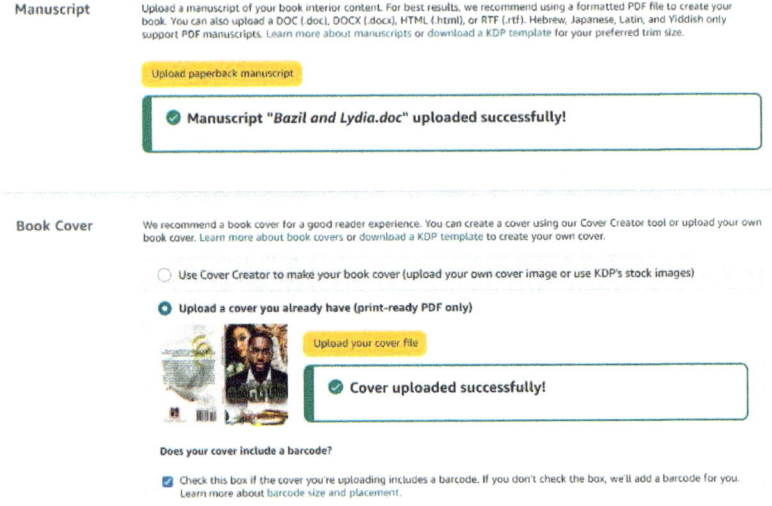

20

Covers, Sizes, & Page Counts on Kindle Direct Publishing (KDP)

If you're happy with the cover you've created, click 'Approve,' scroll down to the bottom of the page, and you'll see the 'Summary' section to the left and 'Your Printing Cost' to the right.

Paperback Rights & Pricing

a. Territories – all territories (worldwide rights) is already highlighted for you.

b. Primary marketplace – I leave my primary marketplace on Amazon.com but you can change it to another location depending on where you located.

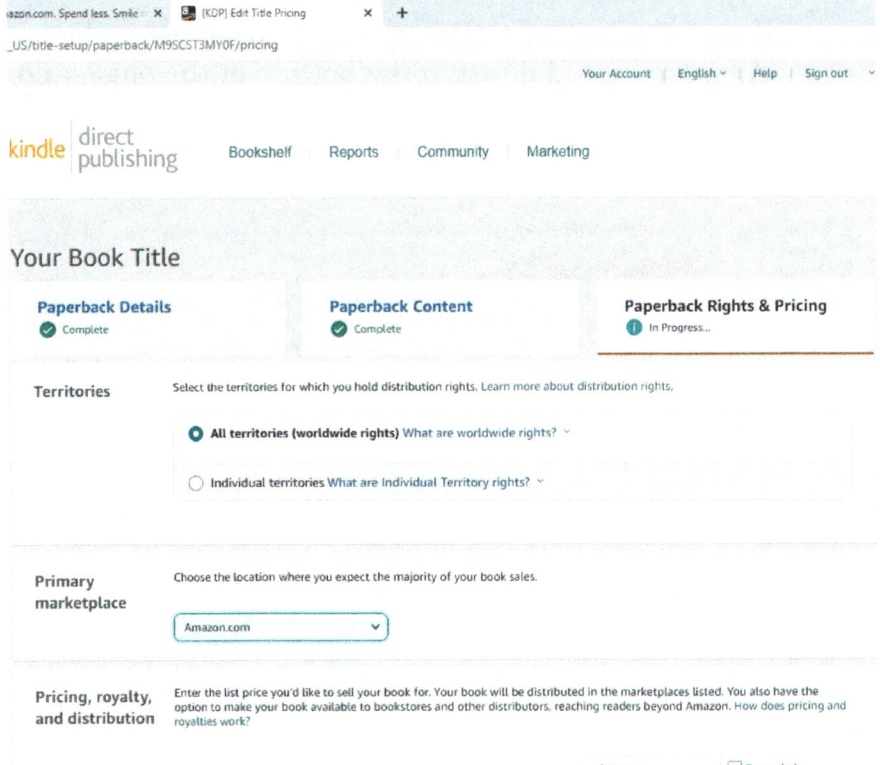

Covers, Sizes, & Page Counts on Kindle Direct Publishing (KDP)

c. Pricing, royalty, and distribution – in this section you'll see the minimum & maximum price you can charge for your book. Make sure you check 'Expanded Distribution' so you can get royalties from all areas. In this example, I put in $15.00 as the price. Your cost is $2.59, your royalty rate is 60%, your royalty is $6.41, your expanded distribution royalty rate is 40%, and your expanded distribution royalty is $3.41. Your cost, royalty rate, and royalties are different in the UK.

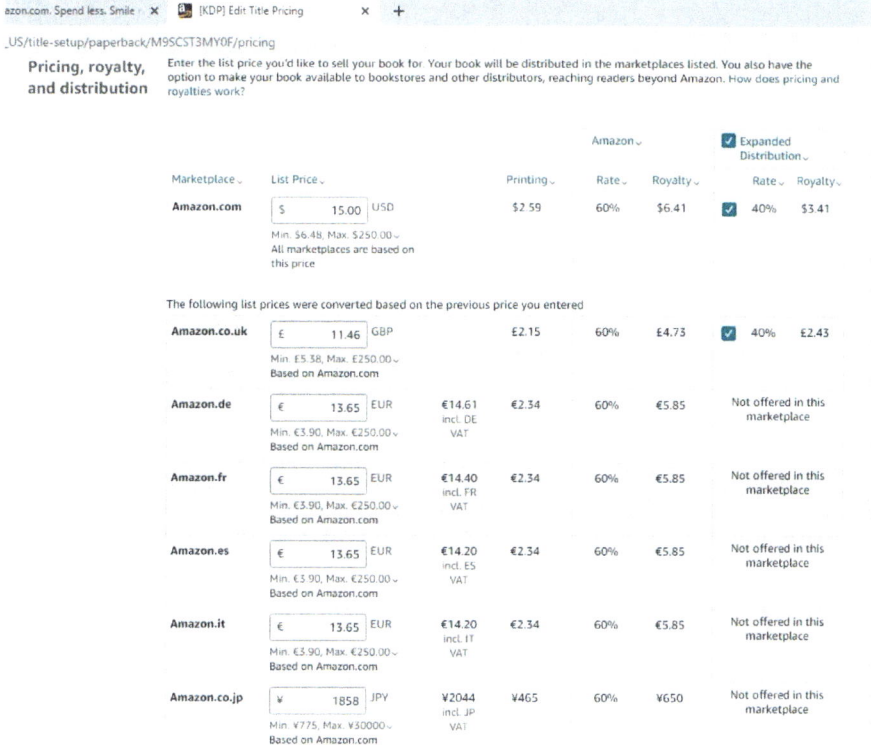

23

Covers, Sizes, & Page Counts on Kindle Direct Publishing (KDP)

d. If you're satisfied with your price, royalty rate, and royalties, scroll down to the bottom of the page and make sure you click 'Request printed proofs of this book!' A message will come up letting you know, 'You have unsaved changes.' Click on 'Save and Continue.'

Covers, Sizes, & Page Counts on Kindle Direct Publishing (KDP)

Click on 'Market Place of Your Order,' put in Amazon.com or your location, and then click 'Submit Proof Request.'

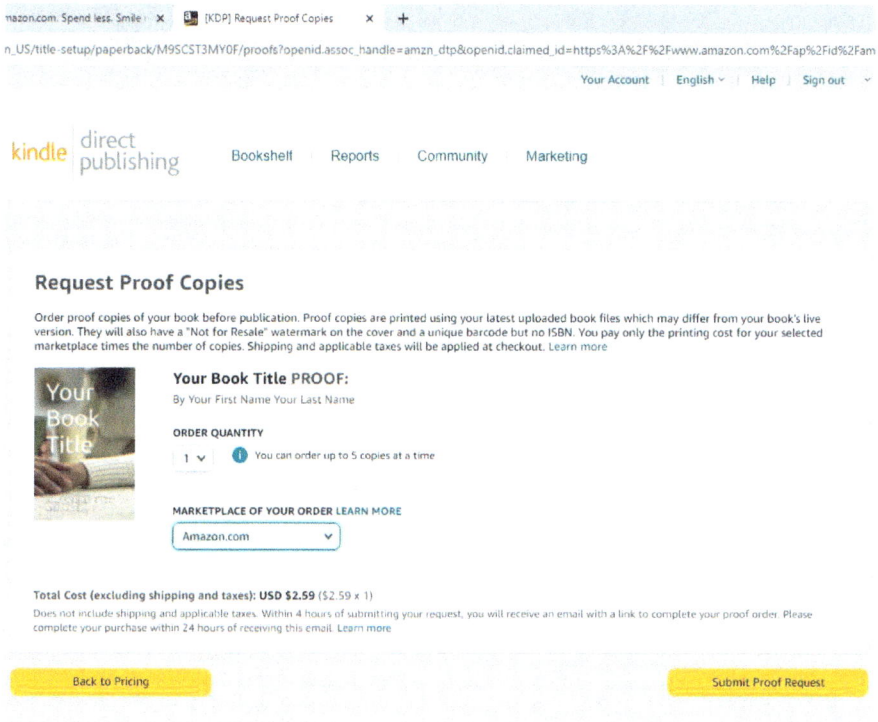

Covers, Sizes, & Page Counts on Kindle Direct Publishing (KDP)

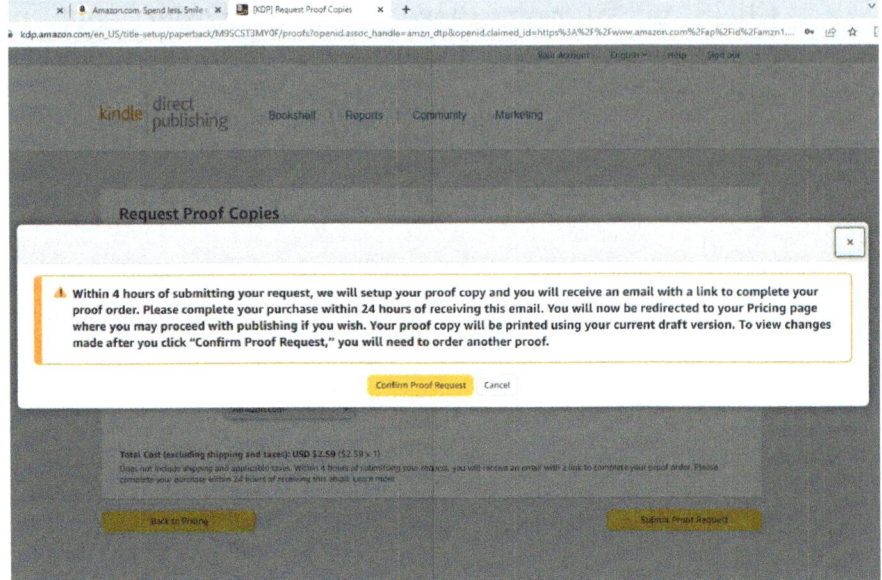

Once you confirm your proof request click 'back to pricing,' scroll to the bottom of the page, and click 'Publish Your Paperback Book.' Amazon will notify you when your book is available.

Covers, Sizes, & Page Counts on Kindle Direct Publishing (KDP)

Book Covers

Covers, Sizes, & Page Counts on Kindle Direct Publishing (KDP)

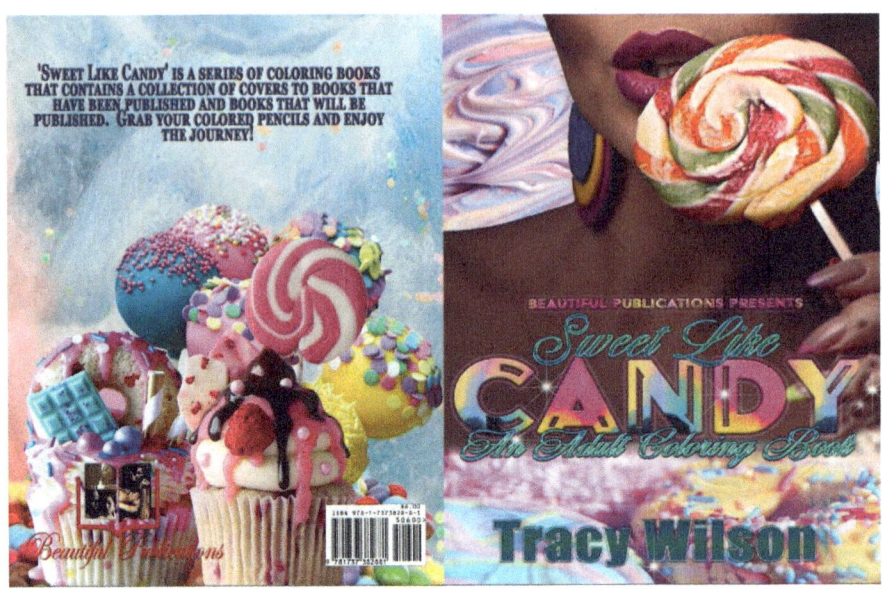

I fell in love with the pre-made eBook cover made by Cyn Alexander when I saw it. It reminded me of a coloring book. I had been thinking about doing a coloring book with my covers for a while and after I saw this eBook cover, I knew I was going to do it. I had a lot of covers and I wanted to add the black & white beside the coloring page so I decided to create a coloring book series and I asked Cyn to create a 2nd eBook cover for me. When I was ready to print, Cyn wasn't doing book covers anymore so I asked Jay Covers to help me create the paperbacks. This is what happens when two great designers come together.

Covers, Sizes, & Page Counts on Kindle Direct Publishing (KDP)

'How Far Are You Willing To Go? Murder Is Just The Beginning' is a crazy, explicit, erotic, psychotic, suspenseful, thrilling, paranormal series. This series takes place in Westchester County, NY. It started with one book and turned into a five-book series. I chose these covers because they look like us, and the nudity represents the vulnerability of the characters. As you read the series, you see that they're completely exposed.

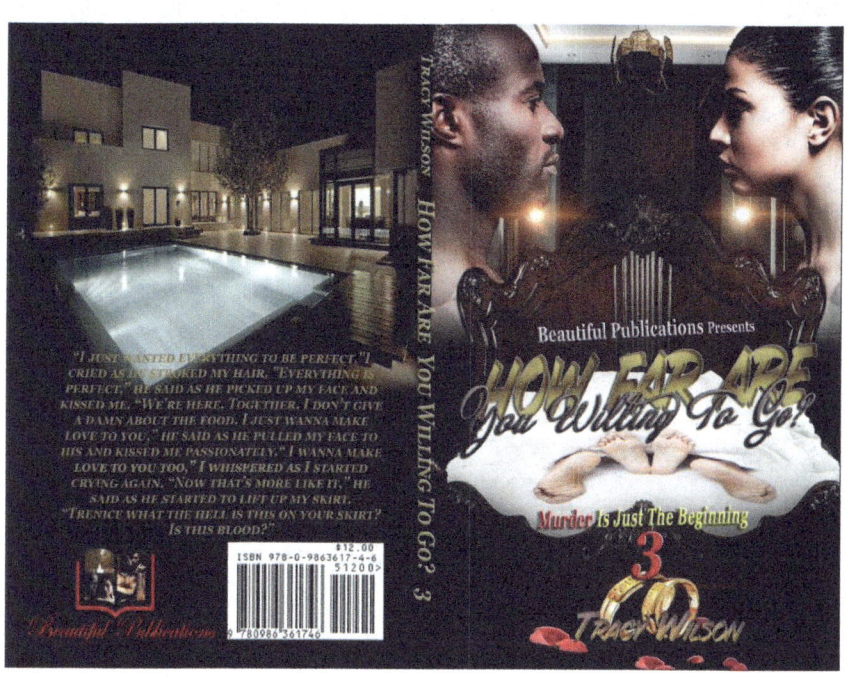

Covers, Sizes, & Page Counts on Kindle Direct Publishing (KDP)

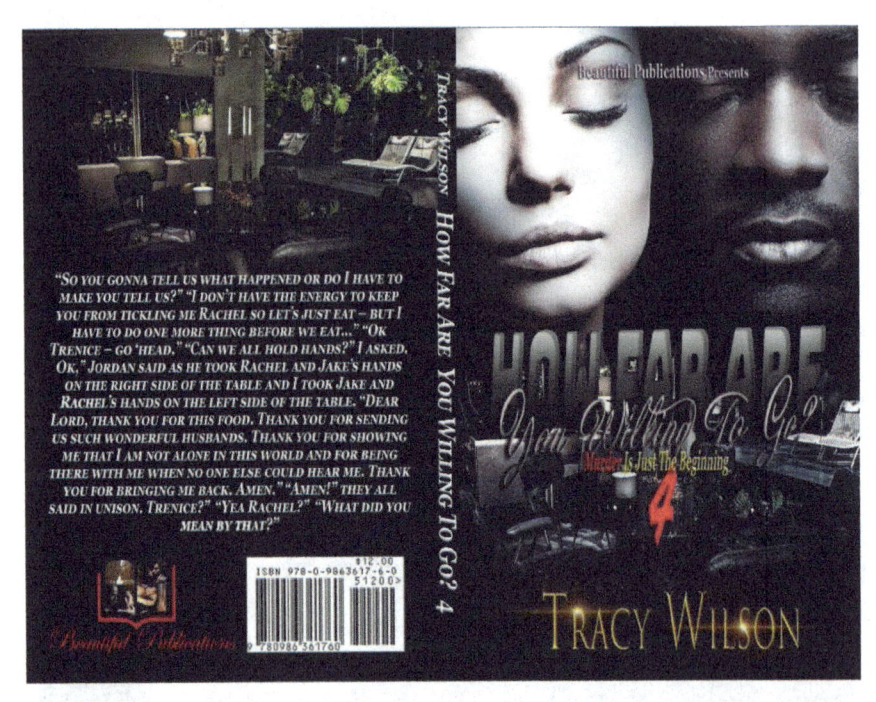

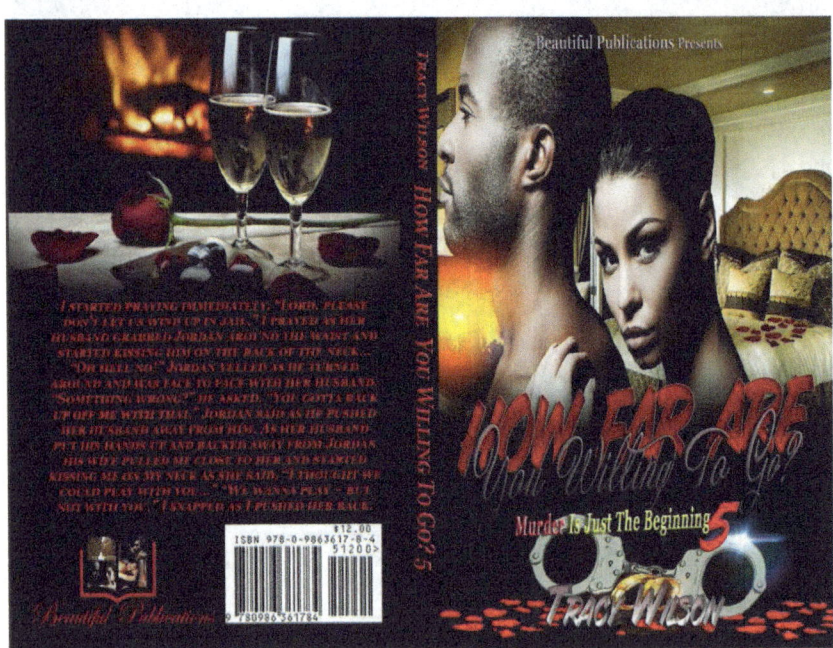

Covers, Sizes, & Page Counts on Kindle Direct Publishing (KDP)

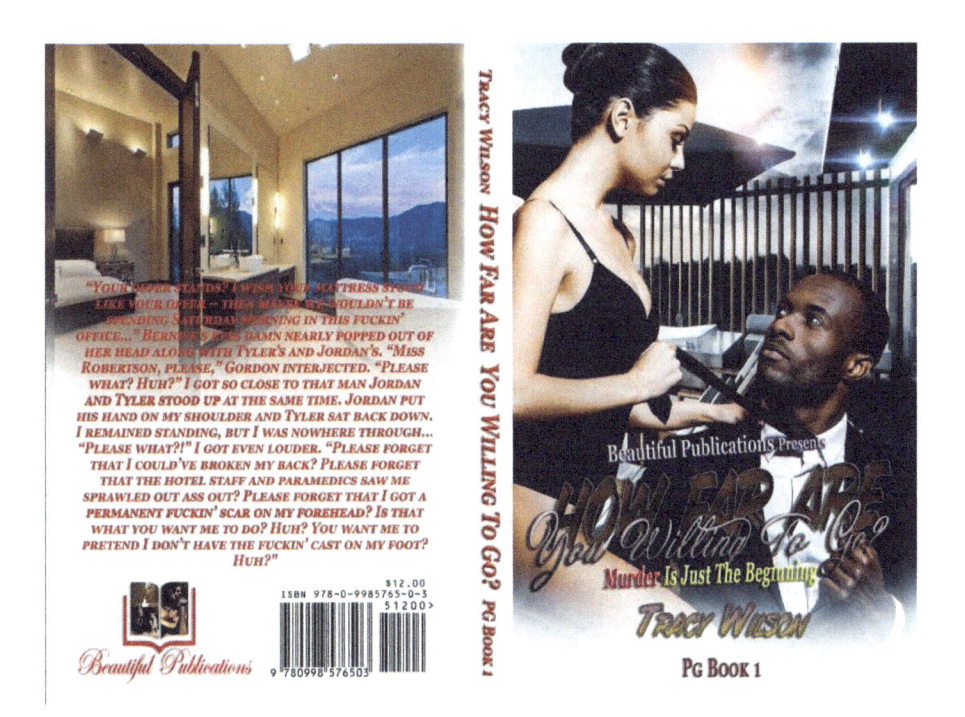

Covers, Sizes, & Page Counts on Kindle Direct Publishing (KDP)

This is the first series I've written that's currently in print in two versions: Explicit & PG. As I was writing the explicit series, my granddaughter wanted to read it so I handed her a few snippets and she asked me if I could write something she could read. I took the five-book series, toned it down, turned it into a three-book series, dedicated it to her, and made her my little sister. This series gives you everything the explicit series gives you but the differences are that the couple is wearing clothes and the books are labeled PG on the bottom of the cover.

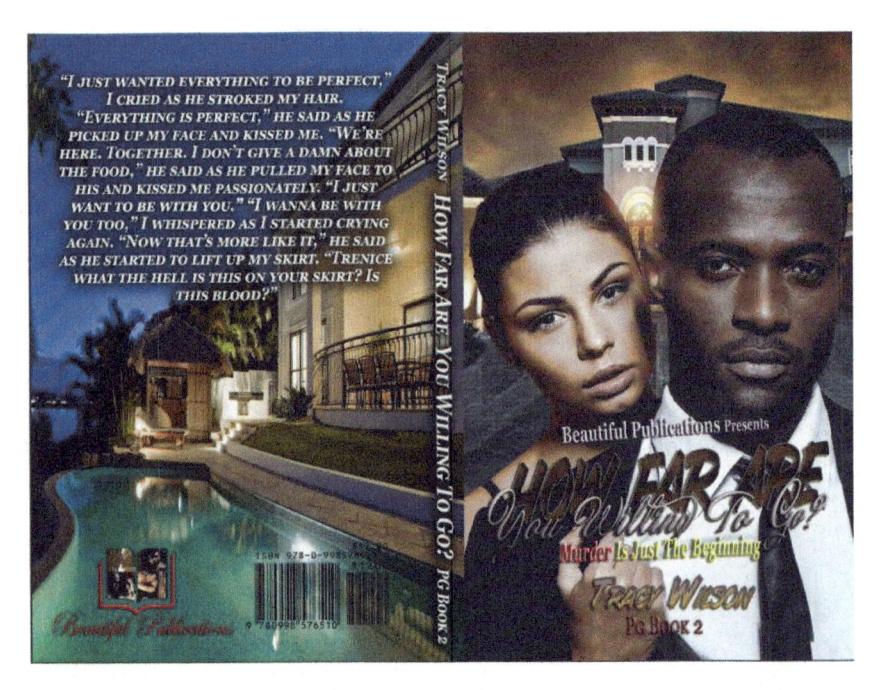

Covers, Sizes, & Page Counts on Kindle Direct Publishing (KDP)

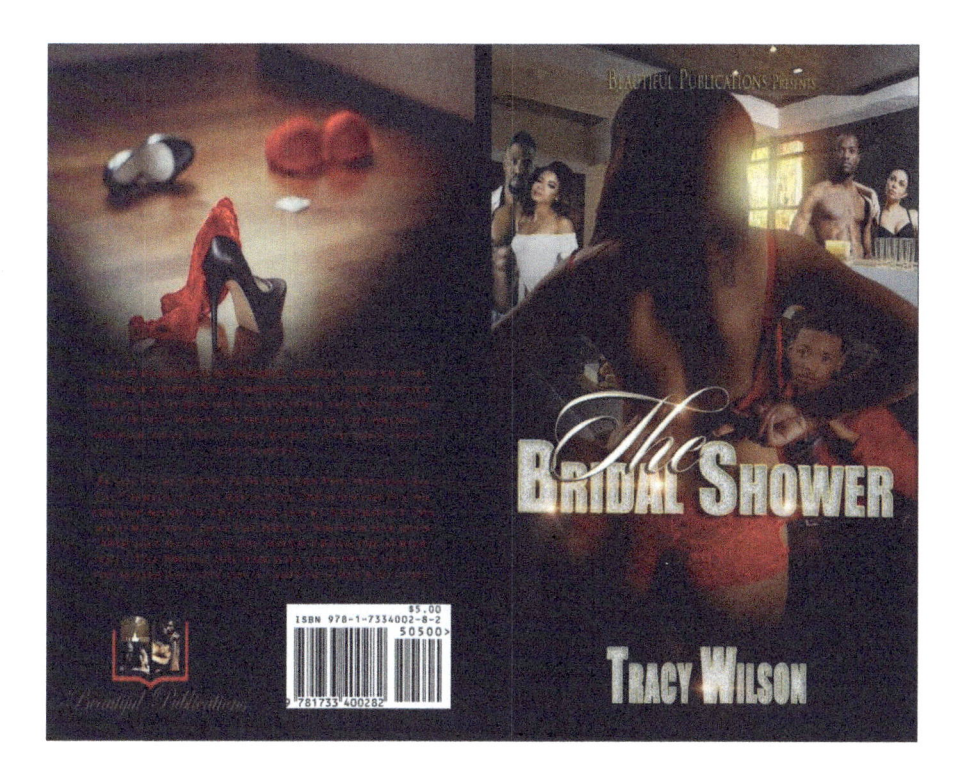

Covers, Sizes, & Page Counts on Kindle Direct Publishing (KDP)

This story was taken from my first series, 'How Far Are You Willing To Go? Murder Is Just The Beginning.' In this story, Trenice makes sure everyone participates whether they like it or not – and they loved it.

'Twisted Series'

After I wrote 'How Far Are You Willing To Go? Murder Is Just The Beginning,' a series that takes place in Westchester County, NY, I wanted to write a series that took place in Fairfield County, CT. I planned to start with my alter-ego, Beautiee, add my brothers, sisters, aunts, uncles, nieces, & nephews, cousins, and 'Twist' them up throughout the series! I used their real names, created jobs for them that fit their personalities, and began writing!

When I was done with the series, I created a 'Twisted Lottery.' I wrote their names on slips of paper, I put their names in a bowl, and I sent each person a book in the series as I drew their names:

Covers, Sizes, & Page Counts on Kindle Direct Publishing (KDP)

Twisted Series Lottery

The Twisted Series
14 books in total – is now complete!

Now that the series is complete, I've entered each of your names into a lottery! The way the lottery works is that everybody wins! 14 books – 1 book for each of you! Your names were written on a piece of paper, put in a vase, and your names were drawn out as follows:

Shireen = Twisted Beautiee 1
Thelma = Twisted Beautiee 2
Cousin Gert = Twisted Beautiee 3
Smalls – Twisted Beautiee 4
Sheila & Henley = Twisted Beautiee 5

Cousin Veronica = Twisted Starr 1
Chandler = Twisted Starr 2
Aunt Crystal = Twisted Starr 3

Marlowe = Twisted Mary 1
Troy & Keisha = Twisted Mary 2
Joselyn & Sam = Twisted Mary 3

Dominique = Twisted Christmas
The Next Generation

Tina = In The Arms Of A Gangster 1
Beautiee's Biography
(As told in Twisted Beautiee)

Uncle Conrad = In The Arms Of A Gangster 2
Beautiee's Biography
(As told in Twisted Beautiee)

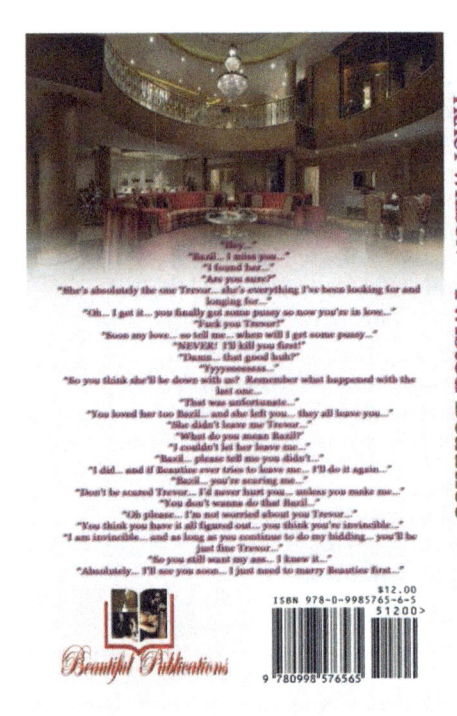

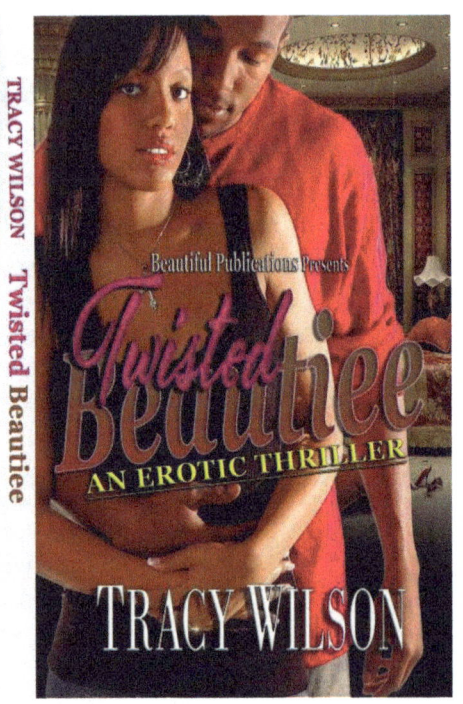

Covers, Sizes, & Page Counts on Kindle Direct Publishing (KDP)

'Twisted Beautiee' is the first set of 5 books in the 14-book 'Twisted Series.' Beautiee meets Bazil and its love-at-first-sight as Bazil falls in love with her. As Beautiee is sitting at the computer planning their wedding in Vegas, Bazil is on the phone with his lover letting him know that he's found the one and needs to marry her ASAP!

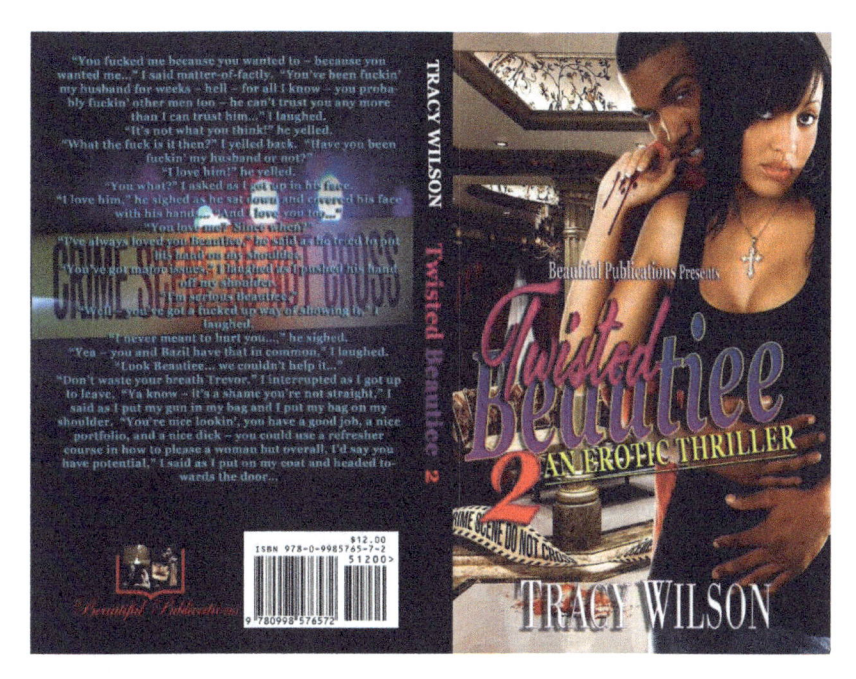

Covers, Sizes, & Page Counts on Kindle Direct Publishing (KDP)

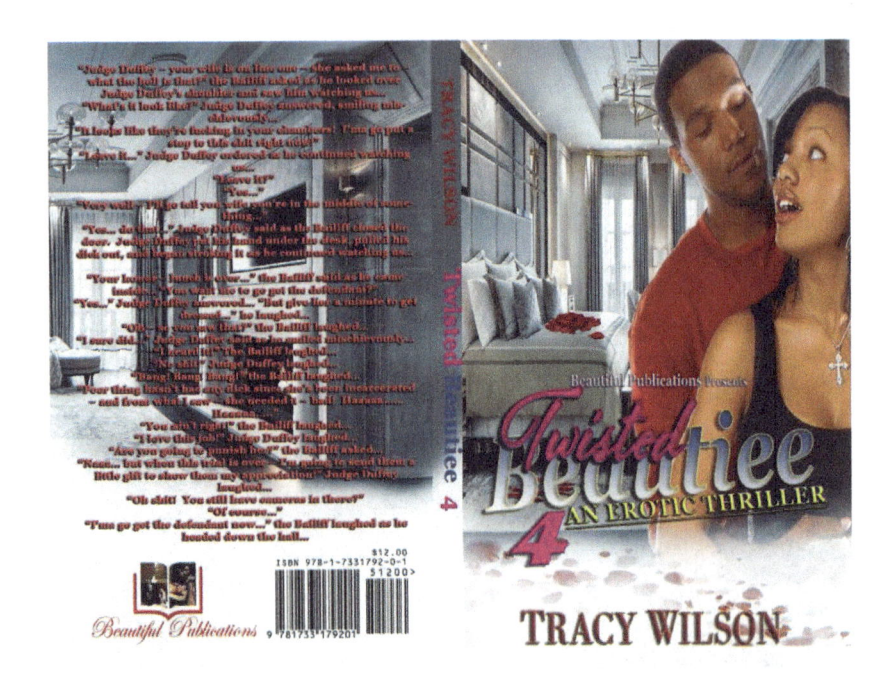

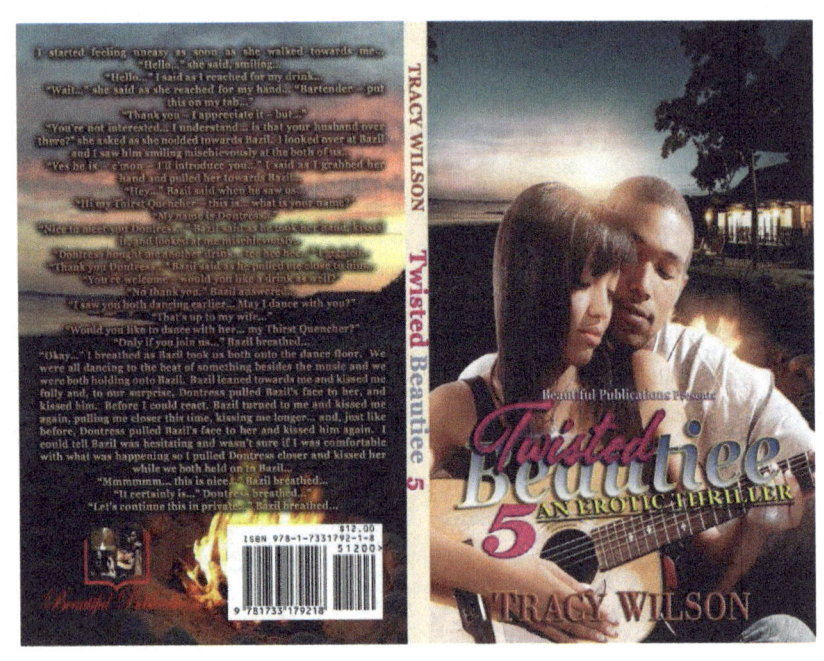

Covers, Sizes, & Page Counts on Kindle Direct Publishing (KDP)

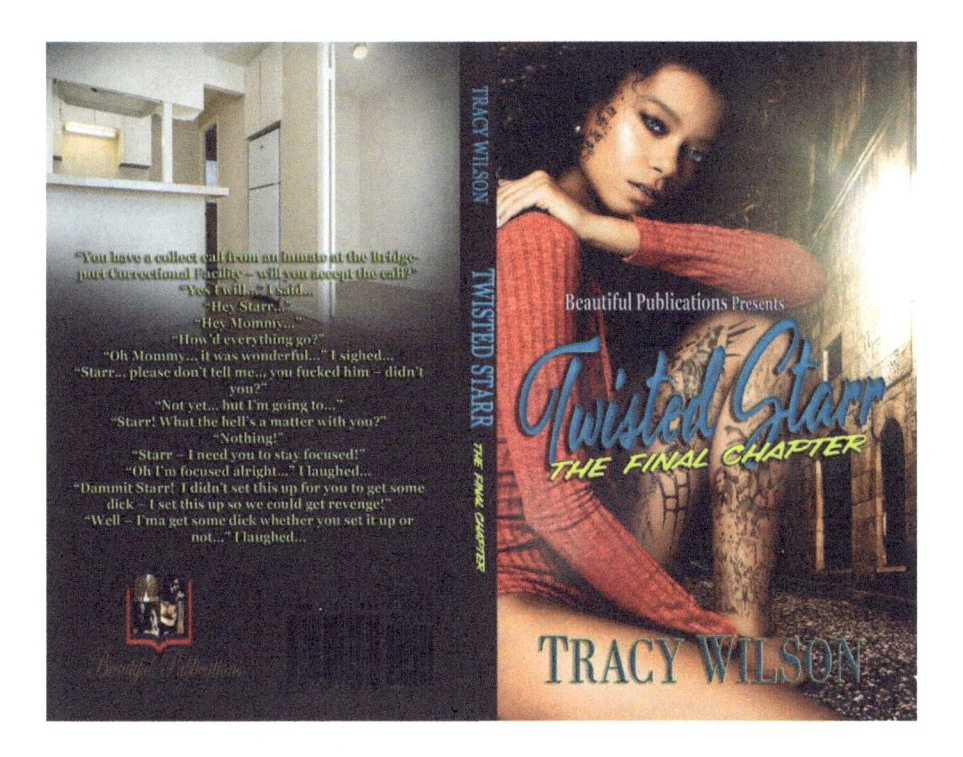

Covers, Sizes, & Page Counts on Kindle Direct Publishing (KDP)

'Twisted Starr' is the second set of 3 books in the 14-book 'Twisted Series.' In this series, Beautiee finds out that Bazil had a daughter with the woman he cheated on his first wife with!

Covers, Sizes, & Page Counts on Kindle Direct Publishing (KDP)

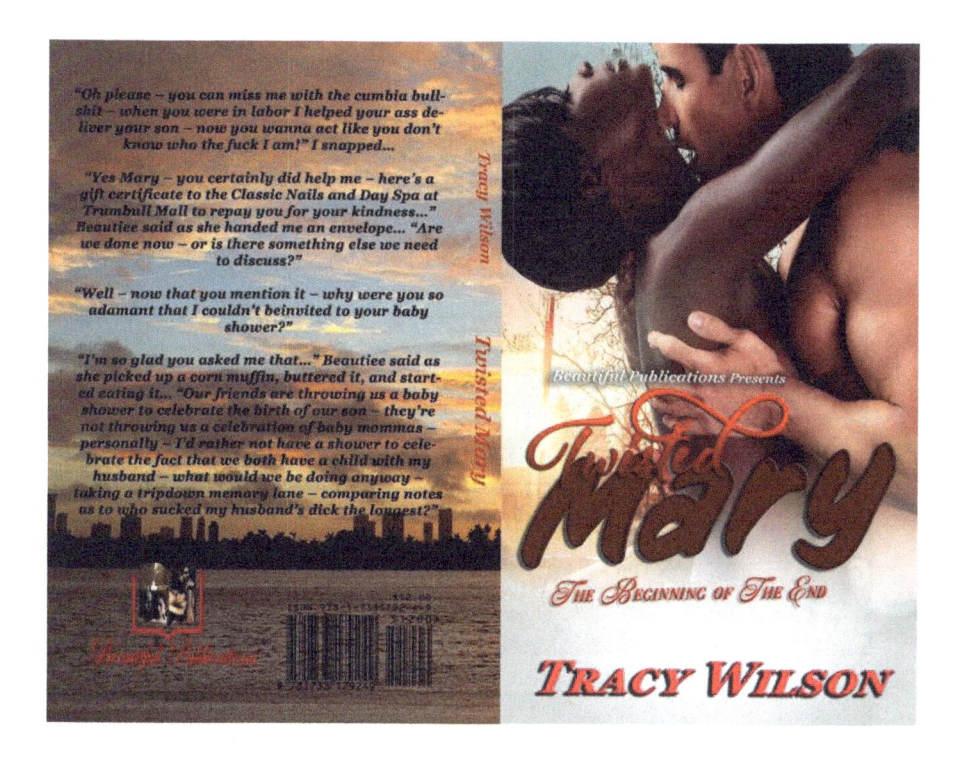

'Twisted Mary' is the third set of 3 books in the 14-book 'Twisted Series.' In this series, Beautiee finds out that Mary is Starr's mother and she also finds out that Bazil knew she was in prison with his daughter's mother and never told her! Mary is determined to make Beautiee's life a living hell because she can't stand the fact that once again, Bazil chose someone else. The only reason Mary lives is because Beautiee loves her daughter!

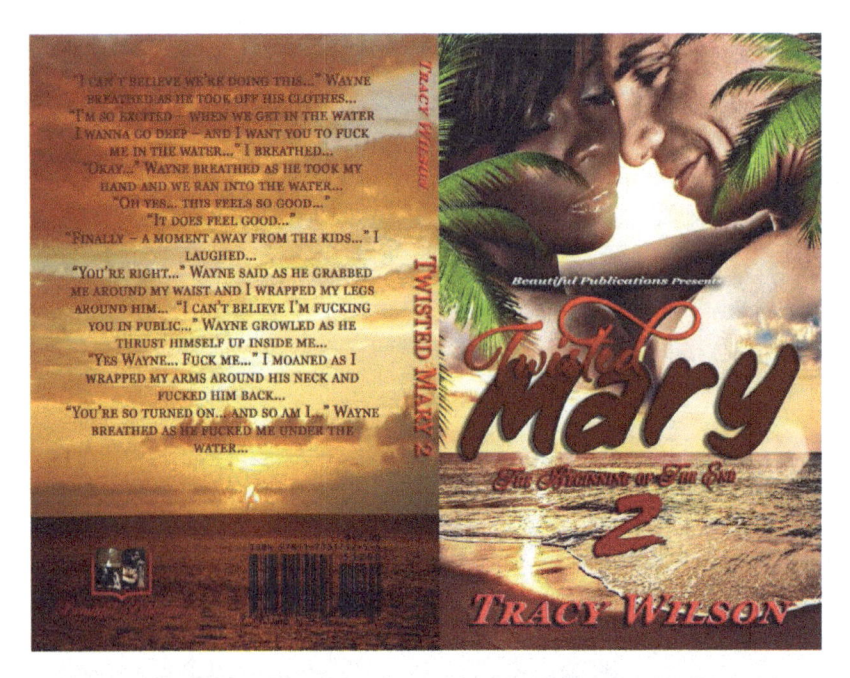

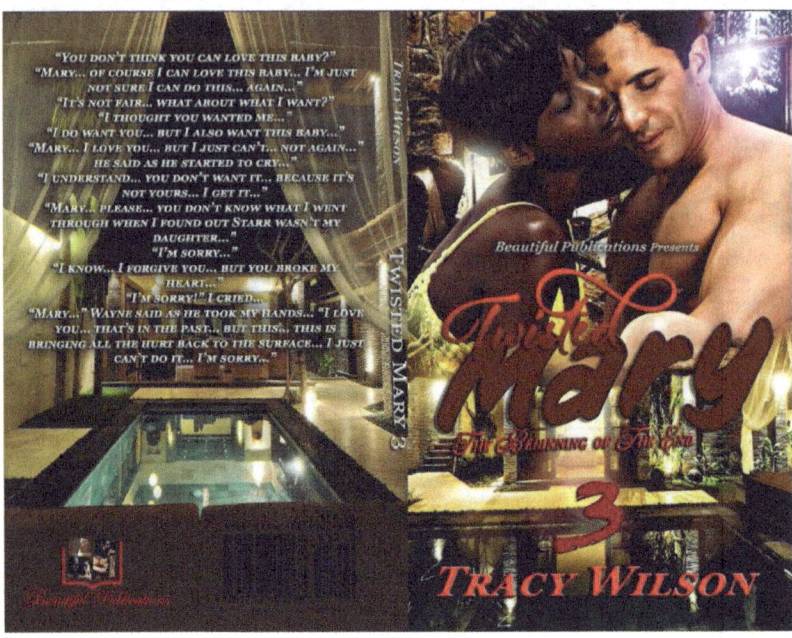

Covers, Sizes, & Page Counts on Kindle Direct Publishing (KDP)

44

Covers, Sizes, & Page Counts on Kindle Direct Publishing (KDP)

'Twisted Christmas - The Next Generation' is all about the children that are born in this 14-book 'Twisted Series.' In this story, everyone goes into labor in different locations at the same time!

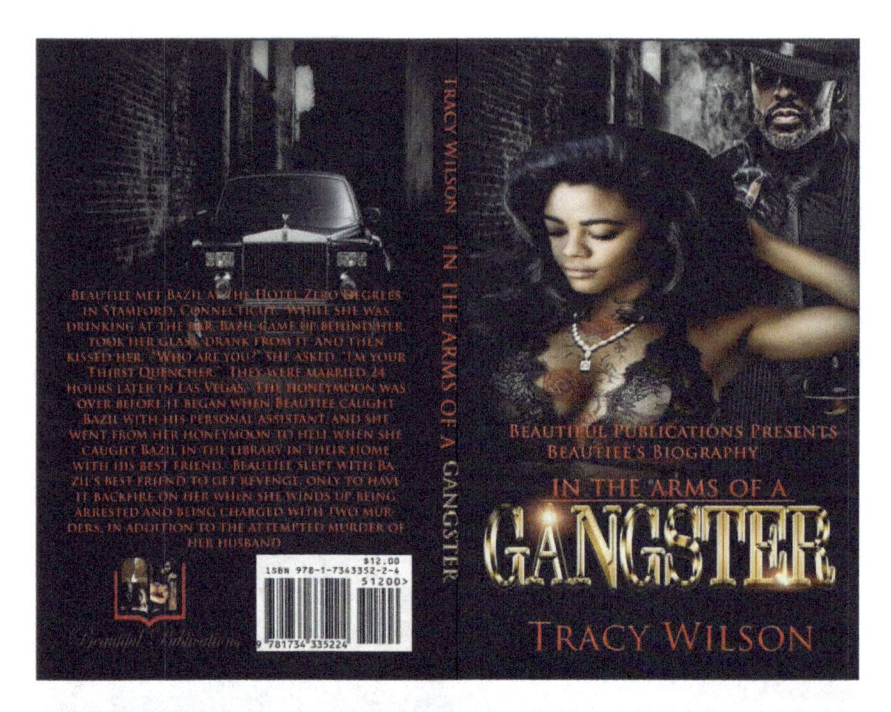

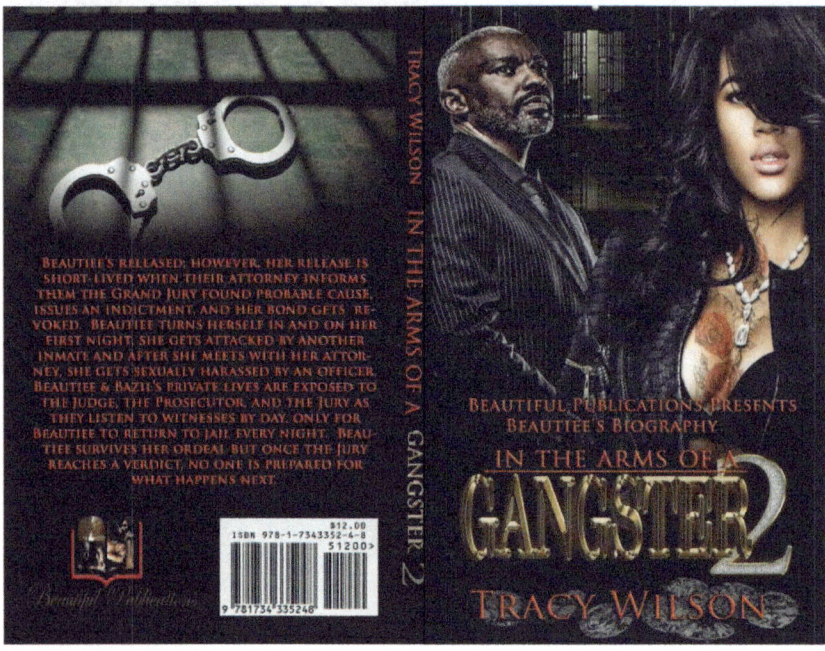

Covers, Sizes, & Page Counts on Kindle Direct Publishing (KDP)

Covers, Sizes, & Page Counts on Kindle Direct Publishing (KDP)

This is the final set of two books in the 14-book 'Twisted Series.' In 'Twisted Beautiee,' Beautiee gets arrested for the attempted murder of her husband, the murder of her lover, and the murder of her husband's lover! Beautiee deals with the trauma of being arrested, going to prison, and the vengeful District Attorney by writing her story after being released.

Covers, Sizes, & Page Counts on Kindle Direct Publishing (KDP)

48

This is the craziest series I have on Amazon to date! I wrote this during the Covid Pandemic. I wanted to write something crazy that would shock you, make you laugh, make you cringe, and make you fall in love - yes – you read that right – I wanted to make you fall in love – with zombies! Ha ha!

The covers for this series have the eBook cover as the back of the paperback cover. That was suggested by my cover designer because I wanted a custom paperback.

This series started with the female zombie on the top paperback cover with the moon. This was a pre-made eBook cover that was on Jay Cover's Facebook page before he had a website. I looked at it, told him I had an idea, and then I asked him if he had any other pictures of the same model. Once he sent me the link, I picked the picture I wanted and then I had to find a picture of Bazil's father so I looked on deposit photos and adobe photos to find a male that would look good as Bazil's father. Once I found the man I was looking for, I asked Jay Covers for the link with the pictures of Bazil & Beautiee from the Twisted Beautiee series, I started looking, and I picked out another picture of the couple. I gave Jay a synopsis of what the story was about and if you look on the covers, you'll see a pile of dirt and you'll also see dirt on Bazil's parents. This is because his parents came back from the dead and came up through that pile of dirt in their backyard!

Bazil & Beautiee get a call from their son's teacher asking to meet with them because she's concerned about a picture their son drew in class. One side of the paper has stick figures of Mommy & Daddy in bed and the other side of the paper has stick figures of monsters coming up out the dirt in the backyard. Bazil & Beautiee laugh when the teacher suggests that perhaps their son hears noises from their bedroom at night that scare him and that's why he drew monsters on the other side of the paper. After meeting with their son's teacher they took their son home and Bazil asked his son to show him where the monsters were coming from. Their son began to tremble and cry as he showed them where the monsters were coming from and that's just the beginning of this crazy story!

As I was writing this story, a friend of mine lost her mother. She would see shadows of her mother outside her window, take pictures, and post them in Facebook. She wasn't afraid at all – she felt that her mother was letting her know she was going to be okay. I reached out to my friend and asked her if she would allow me to use this in my book and she gave me permission to use it in this story.

Covers, Sizes, & Page Counts on Kindle Direct Publishing (KDP)

This is my favorite cover in the 'Erotic Zombies' series. In this series, Beautiee wanted to honor her husband's parents by telling their story. When I got this cover back from my cover designer, I couldn't just let it be a picture of her husband's parents so I came up with the idea to tell the 'Erotic Zombies' story from the parent's point-of-view.

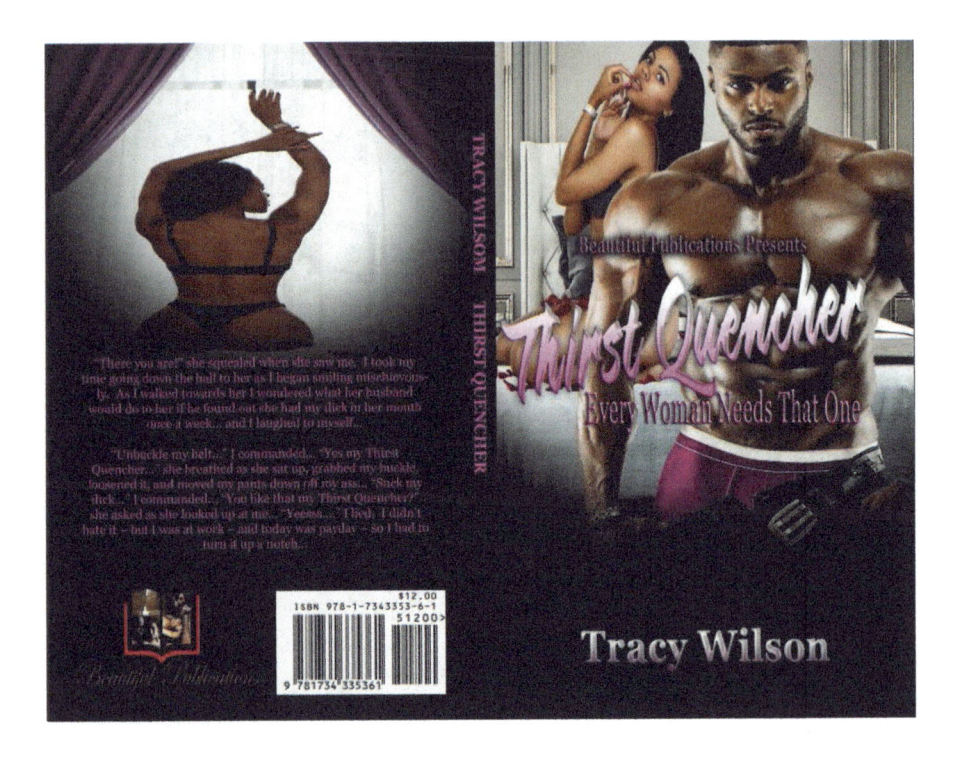

This cover was a pre-made. If you've read the 'Twisted Series' then you're familiar with 'Thirst Quencher.' This story is exactly what you think it is. Fans of this story have asked for more and 'Thirst Quencher: Every Man Needs That One Too' is coming soon.

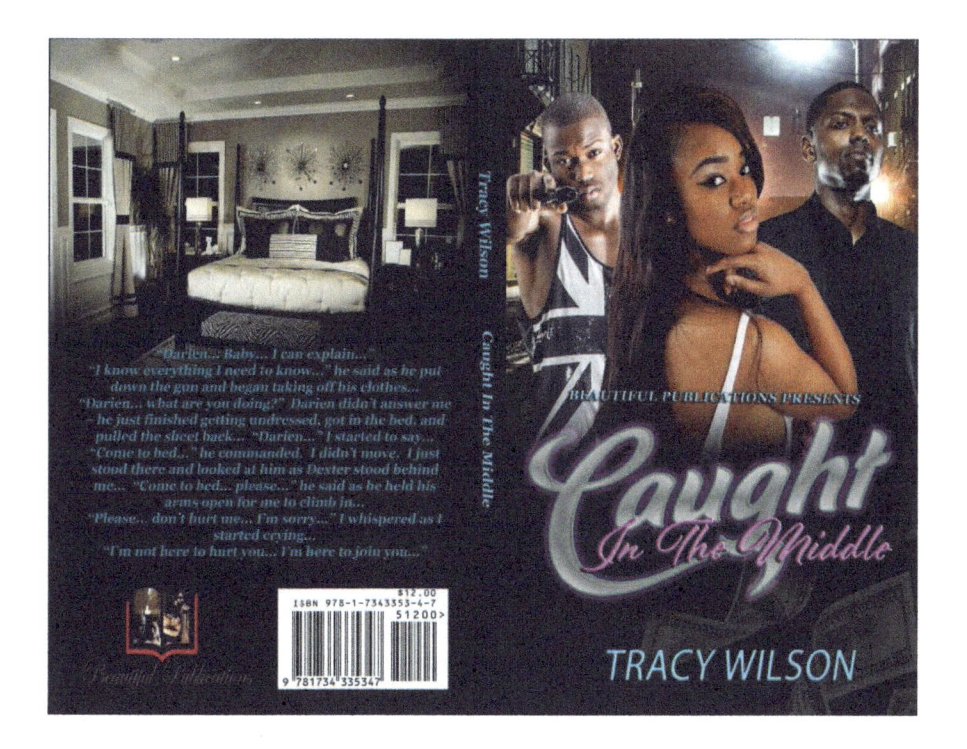

Covers, Sizes, & Page Counts on Kindle Direct Publishing (KDP)

I saw this cover and I didn't want to do the obvious titles like, 'Between Two Men,' 'Two Brothers,' 'My husband and My Lover,' etc. I kept coming up with ideas and as I shared them with my husband, we both decided that 'Caught In The Middle' was the best title for this cover. In this story Lacey gets caught cheating on Darien with Dexter and goes from scared to shock when her Darien puts the gun down, gets undressed, and insists that he be allowed to join them.

This is another crazy, psychotic story! As soon as I saw this pre-made, I knew I was going to write a crazy story. I changed the title because the suggested title went in another direction and I wrote the first chapter of this book the same day. As soon as you start reading this one, you'll realize it's not what it seems... or is it?

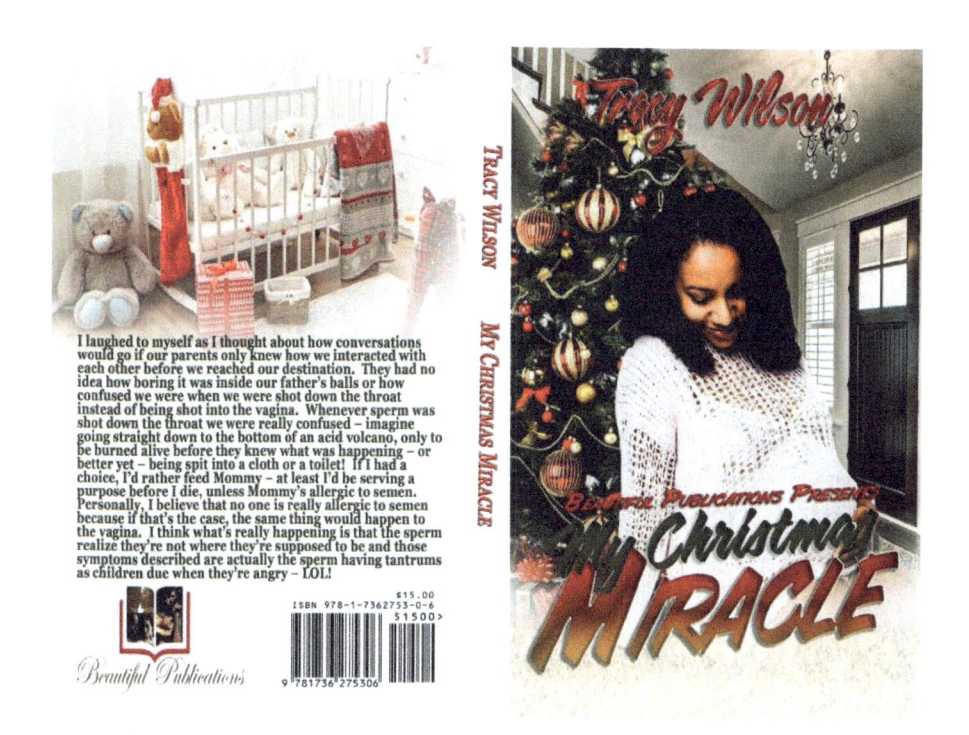

This was a pre-made on Jay Covers' Facebook page. I wasn't sure what the title was going to be but I knew I wanted to write another Christmas story. I decided to make this one rated PG-13 because the story is about a young girl in high school that finds love. This story will make you fall in love with the romance but it will also make you laugh so hard your stomach hurts because the sperm is a major character and the story is told from the unborn baby's point of view!

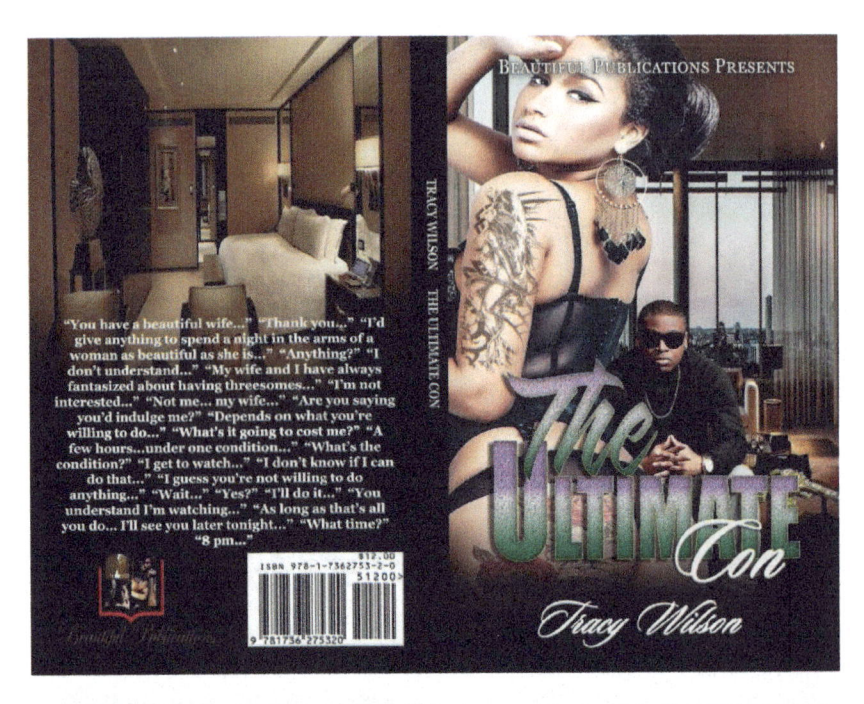

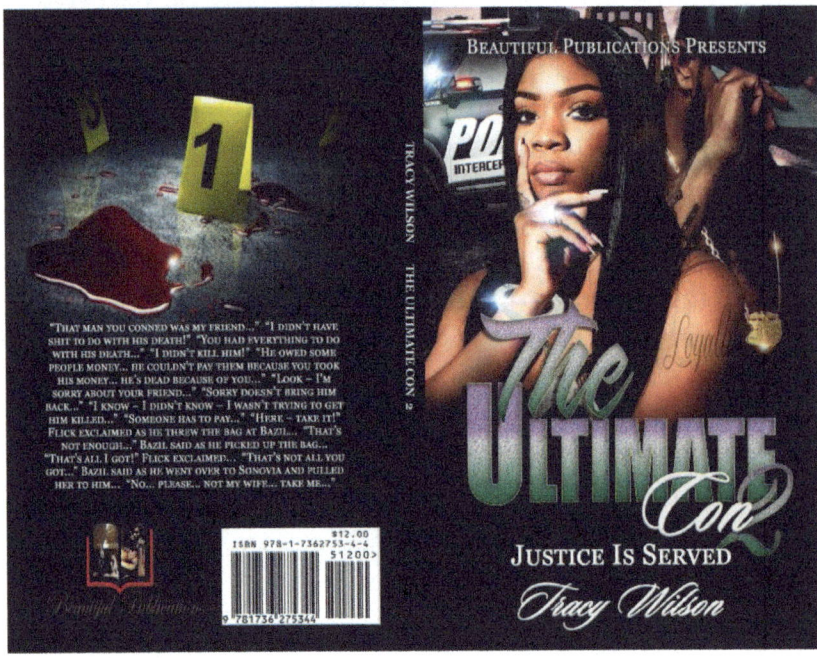

Covers, Sizes, & Page Counts on Kindle Direct Publishing (KDP)

Both of these covers were pre-mades. The 2nd cover was made first. I had a story in mind but decided not to write that story so I held onto the cover. As soon as I saw the 1st cover, I snatched it up before anyone else could buy it. It reminded me of a friend of mine in Facebook, Snow Alexander. I sent her the cover, asked her how she liked it, and told her how much it reminded me of her and her husband. She thanked me for the compliment and told me how much she liked the cover. I was hoping she was open to letting me write a story with her & her husband as main characters and when I told her what the story was about, she was all in! Her husband was even more excited when he found out he was going to be in the book with his wife! I began writing the story and after I sent Snow a few snippets, she messaged me back and asked me if I was going to kill her!

This series takes place in gambling casinos from New York up through Connecticut. Bazil & Beautiee, and Sam, & Joselyn from the 'Twisted Series' are a major part of the story as well as a few new characters. If you like Law & Order Criminal Intent or Casino starring Robert Dinero, Sharon Stone, and Joe Pesci, you'll love this series!

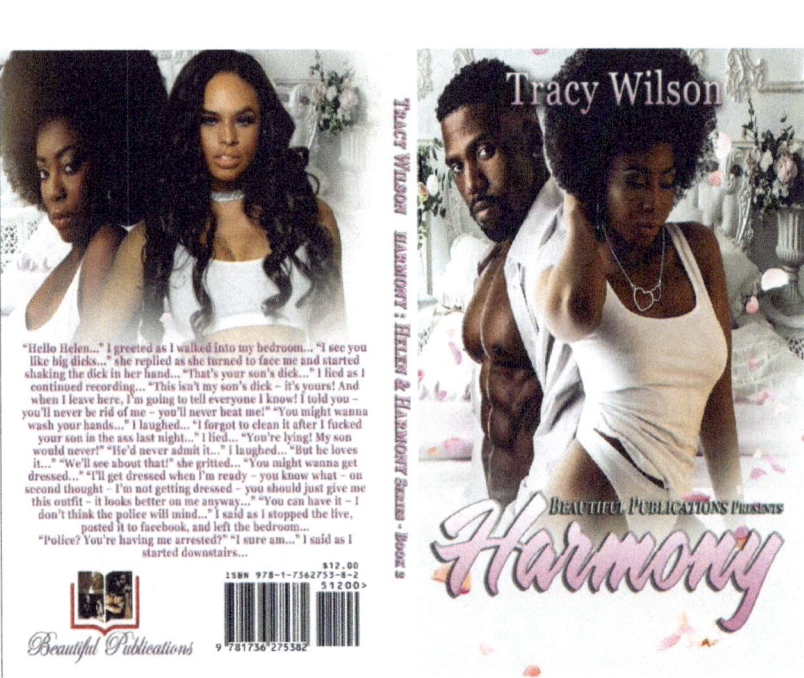

Covers, Sizes, & Page Counts on Kindle Direct Publishing (KDP)

58

This is another crazy, psychotic series! In this series, Harland is forced to choose between his mother, Helen, and his lover, Harmony. You'll have to read this one to find out who he chooses, who lives, and who dies!

I saw the first cover as a pre-made on Jay Cover's website and I thought she would make a good 'Bitch' – Ha ha!

I came up with 'Helen Vs Harmony' after I saw the 2nd cover. Jay was working on it and asked me what I thought of it. As soon as I saw it, I knew I was going to write 'Vs Harmony' – especially because the same man was on both covers!

This series is so crazy and psychotic I had to put a disclaimer at the beginning to let everyone know that I wasn't referring to my mother-in-law!

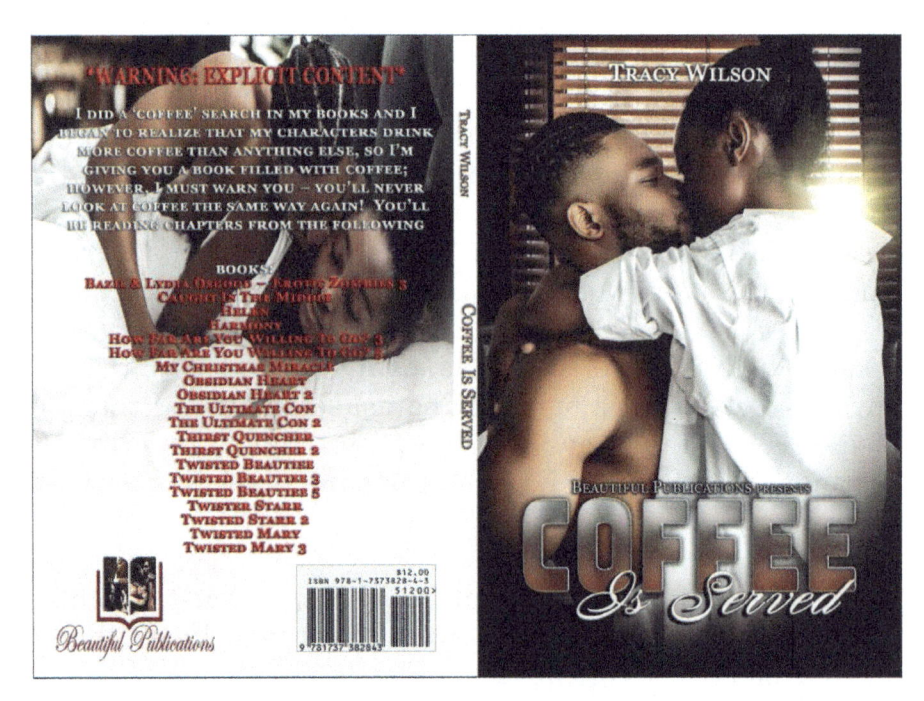

Covers, Sizes, & Page Counts on Kindle Direct Publishing (KDP)

I saw this eBook pre-made and the colors reminded me of coffee. After I came up with the title, I realized how much coffee my characters drink coffee in my books and that's how the 'Coffee Series' was created. The 'Complement' is a custom cover. I came up with the idea for the 'Complement' journal because I'm always networking, I'm always stopping for coffee, and I always need something to write ideas down. This is the first series I created that combines Fiction & Non-Fiction.

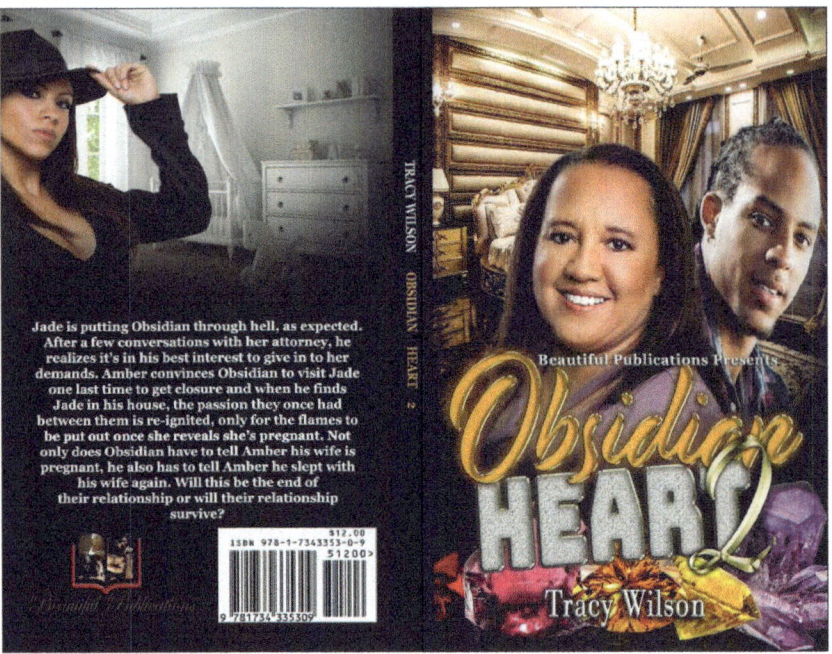

Covers, Sizes, & Page Counts on Kindle Direct Publishing (KDP)

This is fiction but it's based on a true story – it's based on my story. If you've been following me in social media, you know I love crystals, gemstones, spheres, psychics, astrology, and oracle decks. My friend of many years, Chris Varon, was written into this series along with her wife and their dog.

In this series, Jade realizes that Amber is a threat to her marriage and things take a psychotic turn for the worst when she tries to eliminate Amber from this life as she has in a past life. In part two, Jade puts Obsidian through hell as she fights for her marriage and you'll be brought to tears as Obsidian & Amber fight to stay together.

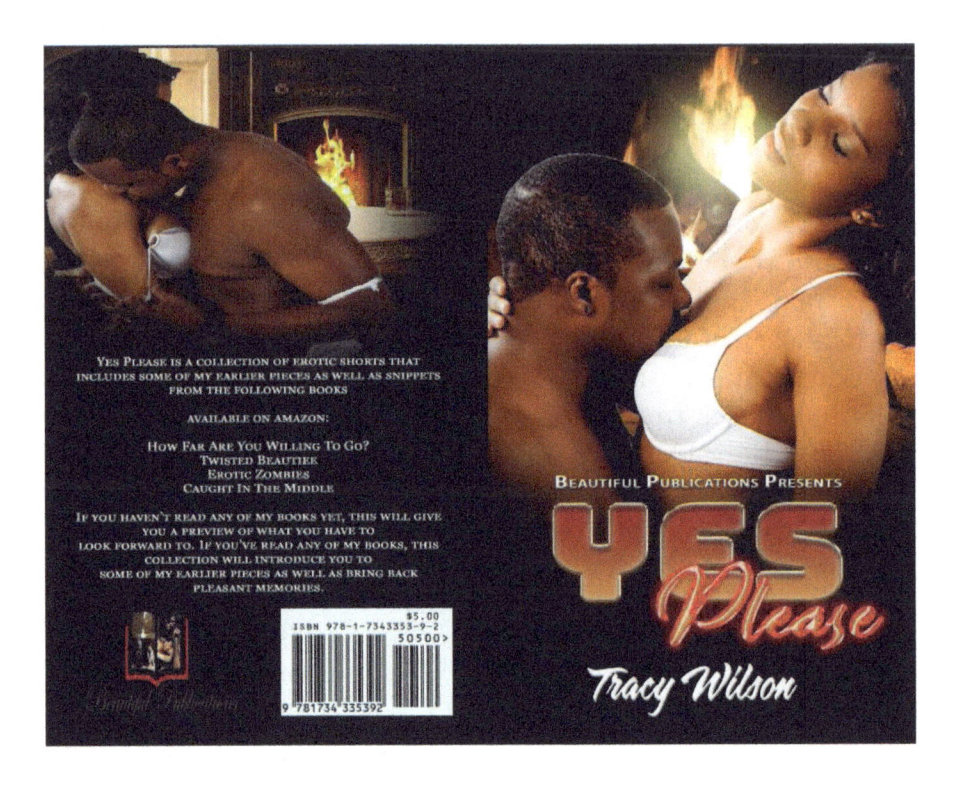

Covers, Sizes, & Page Counts on Kindle Direct Publishing (KDP)

This was a pre-made cover on Jay Cover's Facebook page. I had a collection of erotic shorts that hadn't been published and this cover fit perfectly. I came up with the title after re-reading my erotic shorts.

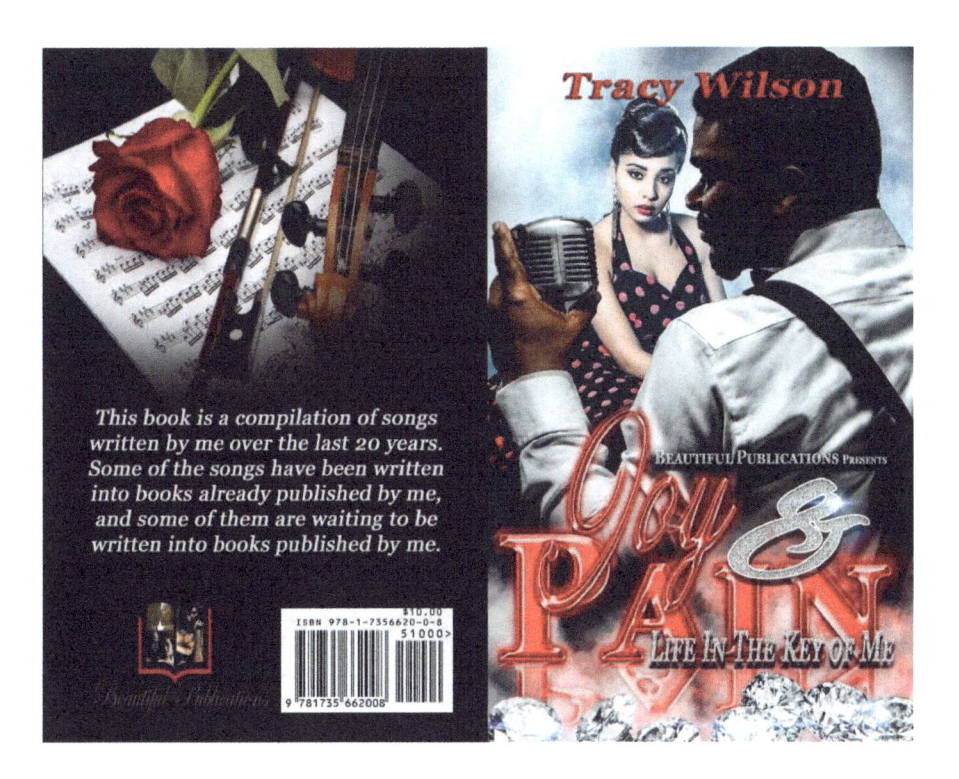

This was a pre-made on Jay Covers' Facebook page. I fell in love with it because it reminds me of me and my husband. We both sing and write songs, and he does the arrangements for my music.

I was going to write a novel based on the original title, but then I thought this cover would be perfect for my songs so I changed the title and sent the book to Cyn Alexander to create an eBook with custom headers. Go look this one up on amazon and take a look inside. The headers are so beautiful.

Covers, Sizes, & Page Counts on Kindle Direct Publishing (KDP)

This is a custom cover. Each time I do an event, I get asked how to write a book. I wrote this book to get you motivated and get you writing.

Covers, Sizes, & Page Counts on Kindle Direct Publishing (KDP)

This is a custom cover. I sent 'Turn Your Story Into A Beautiful Publication' to Cyn Alexander to create an eBook with custom headers. I loaded the epub file into calibre and it wasn't aligned the way I wanted it. It's easy when you write fiction but when it comes to non-fiction, it's extremely challenging. Cyn hadn't ever had a situation like this so I sat down at the computer and began editing the html code that I was familiar with from when I was a tournament director in the MSN Gaming Zone. As soon as I realized I was able to fix it, I knew I had to write a book showing people how to read html code. When I started writing, I never thought I would write a book teaching people how to read html code!

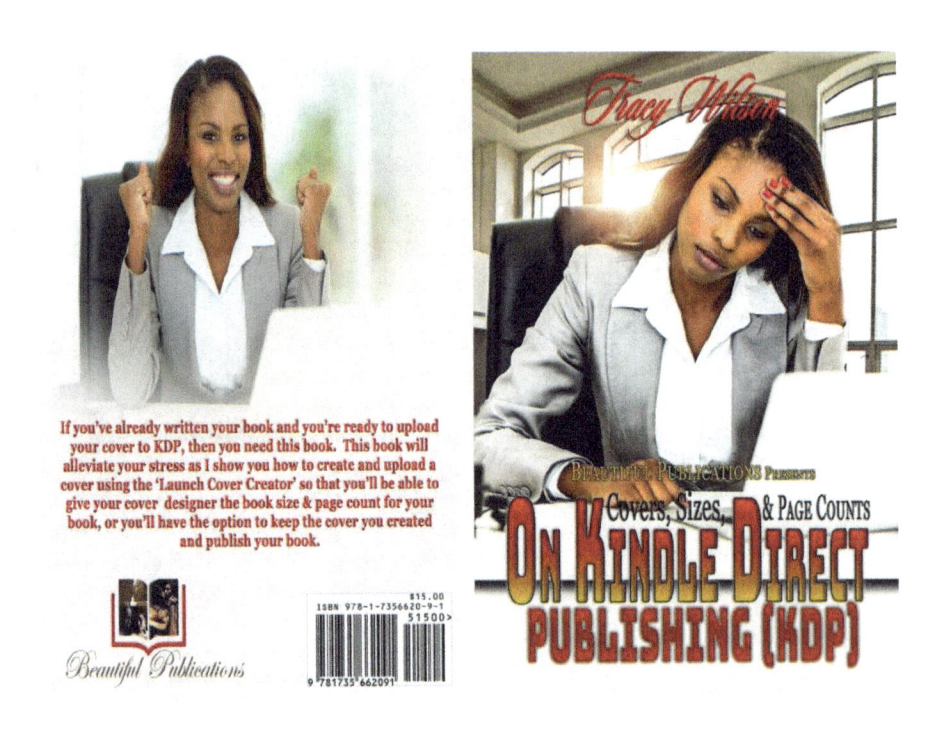

Covers, Sizes, & Page Counts on Kindle Direct Publishing (KDP)

This is a custom cover. I wanted a cover designed to let you know I understand how frustrating and challenging it can be when you don't understand the process. I wrote this book to help you get your cover on Kindle Direct Publishing (KDP) and publish your book.

Made in the USA
Coppell, TX
18 April 2022